The April 2015 Senior Loan Officer Opinion Survey on Bank Lending Practices addressed changes in the standards and terms on, and demand for, bank loans to businesses and households over the past three months.[1] This summary discusses the responses from 76 domestic banks and 23 U.S. branches and agencies of foreign banks.[2]

Regarding loans to businesses, the April survey results indicated that, on balance, banks reported little change in their standards on commercial and industrial (C&I) loans in the first quarter of 2015.[3] On net, banks reported having eased some price terms. With respect to commercial real estate (CRE) lending, on balance, survey respondents reported having eased standards on loans secured by nonfarm nonresidential properties. A few large banks also indicated that they had eased standards on construction and land development loans, and some large banks reported that they had eased standards on loans secured by multifamily properties.[4] In addition, survey respondents reported having eased some CRE loan terms, on net, over the past year. On the demand side, banks indicated having experienced little change in demand for C&I loans in the first quarter; in contrast, respondents reported stronger demand for all three categories of CRE loans covered in the survey.

The survey contained a set of special questions about lending to firms in the oil and natural gas drilling or extraction sector. Banks expected delinquency and charge-off rates on such loans to deteriorate over 2015, but they indicated that their exposures were small, and that they were undertaking a number of actions to mitigate the risk of loan losses.

Regarding loans to households, banks reported having eased lending standards for a number of categories of residential mortgage loans over the past three months on net. Most banks reported no change in standards and terms on consumer loans. On the demand side, moderate net fractions of banks reported stronger demand across most categories of home-purchase loans. Similarly, respondents experienced stronger demand for auto and credit card loans on balance.

---

[1] Respondent banks received the survey on or after March 31, 2015, and responses were due by April 14, 2015.

[2] Unless otherwise indicated, this document refers to reports from domestic banks in the survey.

[3] For questions that ask about lending standards or terms, reported net fractions equal the fraction of banks that reported having tightened ("tightened considerably" or "tightened somewhat") minus the fraction of banks that reported having eased ("eased considerably" or "eased somewhat"). For questions that ask about loan demand, reported net fractions equals the fraction of banks that reported stronger demand ("substantially stronger" or "moderately stronger") minus the fraction of banks that reported weaker demand ("substantially weaker" or "moderately weaker").

[4] The three categories of CRE loans covered in the survey are construction and land development loans, loans secured by nonfarm nonresidential properties, and loans secured by multifamily residential properties.

Lending to Businesses
(Table 1, questions 1–18; Table 2, questions 1–14)

Questions on commercial and industrial lending. Banks reported little change in standards for C&I loans to firms of all sizes over the past three months, as the small number of banks that reported having tightened standards about equaled the small number that reported having eased them.[5] Moderate net fractions of banks continued to report having narrowed spreads, including interest rate floors less frequently, and reducing the cost of credit lines; a modest net fraction of banks reduced the premium charged on riskier loans to large and middle-market firms. Banks generally indicated that they had left nonprice terms about unchanged, although modest net fractions of banks reported having eased policies on loan covenants and having increased the maximum size of credit lines. A few foreign banks reported having eased standards on C&I loans, and modest net fractions of such banks indicated they had increased the maximum size of credit lines or decreased the use of loan covenants.

Most domestic respondents that reported having eased either standards or terms on C&I loans over the past three months cited more-aggressive competition from other banks or nonbank lenders as an important reason for having done so. Smaller numbers of banks also attributed their easing to a more favorable or less uncertain economic outlook, increased tolerance for risk, or improvements in industry-specific problems.

The small number of banks that reported having tightened either their standards or terms on C&I loans predominantly pointed to industry-specific problems, a less favorable or more uncertain economic outlook, or increased concerns about the effects of legislative changes, supervisory actions, or changes in accounting standards as the main reasons for having tightened their lending policies to nonfinancial businesses.

Responses about demand for C&I loans were mixed, and, on balance, demand was little changed over the first quarter of 2015. Those banks that reported having seen stronger demand primarily attributed it to increased investment in plant or equipment, increased financing needs for accounts receivable, increased financing needs for inventories, increased funding needs for mergers or acquisitions, or a shift of customer borrowing to their bank from other bank or nonbank sources. Banks that reported having experienced weaker demand pointed to decreased need for merger or acquisition financing, a shift of customer borrowing away from their bank to other bank and nonbank sources, decreased investment in plant or equipment, and increases in customer internally generated funds. The large majority of foreign banks reported having experienced little change in loan demand over the first quarter of 2015.

Special questions on commercial and industrial lending. The April survey asked a set of special questions about lending to firms in the oil and natural gas drilling or extraction sector. Of the banks that made loans to such firms, more than 80 percent indicated that such lending accounted for less than

---

[5] The survey asked respondents separately about their standards for, and demand from, large and middle-market firms, which are generally defined as firms with annual sales of $50 million or more, and small firms, which are those with annual sales of less than $50 million.

10 percent of their C&I loans outstanding. More than half of the banks who made loans to this sector expected loan quality to deteriorate somewhat over the remainder of 2015. Banks indicated they were taking a variety of actions to mitigate loan losses, including restructuring outstanding loans, reducing the size of existing credit lines, requiring additional collateral, tightening underwriting policies on new loans or lines of credit, and enforcing material adverse change clauses or other covenants.

Questions on commercial real estate lending. On balance, survey respondents reported having eased standards on loans secured by nonfarm nonresidential properties. A few large banks indicated that they had eased standards on construction and land development loans, and some large banks reported that they had eased standards on loans secured by multifamily properties. Regarding changes in demand for CRE loans, modest net fractions of banks indicated that they had experienced stronger demand for loans secured by multifamily residential properties and loans secured by nonfarm nonresidential properties. A somewhat larger net fraction of banks reported stronger demand for construction and land development loans. Foreign respondents reported little change to either standards on, or demand for, CRE loans.

Special questions on commercial real estate lending. The April survey included a set of special questions (repeated annually, with some differences, since 2001) regarding changes in specific lending policies for CRE loans over the past year. Moderate net fractions of banks reported that, over the past 12 months, they had eased spreads, increased maximum loan sizes, and increased the maximum maturity on such loans; a modest net fraction indicated that they had increased market areas served. Survey respondents did not report many changes in other loan terms, such as loan-to-value ratios and debt service coverage ratios. Several foreign respondents reported having decreased spreads over the past year, while few reported changes in other terms.

Survey respondents were asked to rank the top four reasons for their changes in lending policies. Both domestic and foreign banks primarily pointed to more-aggressive competition from other bank or nonbank lenders and more favorable or less uncertain outlooks for vacancy rates or CRE property prices.

Finally, banks were asked how they expected the pace of CRE loan originations during 2015 to change relative to 2014. A modest net fraction of domestic banks and a few foreign banks expected an increase in the pace of originations for loans secured by nonfarm nonresidential properties. In addition, domestic banks also expected the pace of one- to four-family residential construction loans to increase somewhat during 2015 relative to 2014. In contrast, the expected paces of originations for the remaining categories of CRE loans were about unchanged for both domestic and foreign respondents.

Lending to Households
(Table 1, questions 19–33)

Questions on residential real estate lending. Modest net fractions of banks indicated that they had eased standards on loans eligible for purchase by government-sponsored enterprises (known as GSE-eligible mortgage loans) and on government and qualified mortgage (QM) jumbo mortgage loans.[6] Regarding changes in demand, modest to moderate net fractions of banks reported stronger demand across most categories of home-purchase loans. Modest net fractions of banks reported having eased their standards on, and experienced stronger demand for, home equity lines of credit.

Special questions on residential real estate lending. A special question asked banks about how they had responded to new guidelines issued by the GSEs on November 20, 2014, on the definition of life-of-loan representation and warranty exclusions. These policies were designed, in part, to reduce uncertainty and increase transparency about the conditions under which securitized mortgages would be returned to the bank that originated the loan.[7] Only a few banks indicated that they had changed their lending policies in response to the new guidelines.

Questions on consumer lending. A small net fraction of large banks indicated that they were more willing to make consumer installment loans over the past three months. A few large banks reported having eased their standards for auto loans and for consumer loans other than credit card and auto loans, while standards for approving applications for credit card loans were about unchanged on net. Moreover, most terms on credit cards were reported to have changed little. Very few banks reported changes on any of the terms on auto loans or other consumer loans, except for a small net fraction of banks that reported having reduced the spreads of loan rates over the cost of funds for both loan types.

A modest net fraction of large banks reported having experienced an increase in demand for credit cards over the past three months; a modest net fraction of smaller banks indicated having seen stronger demand for auto loans. In contrast, demand for other consumer loans was reported to have remained about unchanged.

This document was prepared by John Driscoll, with the assistance of Shaily Patel, Division of Monetary Affairs, Board of Governors of the Federal Reserve System.

---

[6] See the appendix for a description of the seven categories of residential home-purchase loans introduced in the January 2015 survey.

[7] For the text of the announcement, see Fannie Mae (2014), "Lender Selling Representations and Warranties Framework Updates," *Selling Guide* announcement SEL-2014-14, November 20, available at www.fanniemae.com/portal/funding-the-market/mbs/news/2014/announcement-112014.html.

Appendix: Definitions

The January 2015 survey introduced new categories of residential real estate (RRE) loans that were designed to reflect the Consumer Financial Protection Bureau's qualified mortgage rules.[8] The seven new categories of RRE loans are defined as follows:

1. The **GSE-eligible** category of residential mortgages includes loans that meet the underwriting guidelines, including the loan limit amounts, of the government-sponsored enterprises (GSEs) Fannie Mae and Freddie Mac.

2. The **government** category of residential mortgages includes loans that are insured by the Federal Housing Administration, guaranteed by the Department of Veterans Affairs, or originated under government programs, including the U.S. Department of Agriculture home loan programs.

3. The **QM non-jumbo, non-GSE-eligible** category of residential mortgages includes loans that satisfy the standards for a qualified mortgage and have loan balances that are below the loan limit amounts set by the GSEs but otherwise do not meet the GSE underwriting guidelines.

4. The **QM jumbo** category of residential mortgages includes loans that satisfy the standards for a qualified mortgage but have loan balances that are above the loan limit amount set by the GSEs.

5. The **non-QM jumbo** category of residential mortgages includes loans that do not satisfy the standards for a qualified mortgage and have loan balances that are above the loan limit amount set by the GSEs.

6. The **non-QM non-jumbo** category of residential mortgages includes loans that do not satisfy the standards for a qualified mortgage and have loan balances that are below the loan limit amount set by the GSEs. Banks were asked to exclude from this category loans classified as subprime.

---

[8] The definition of a qualified mortgage (QM) was introduced in the 2013 Mortgage Rules under the Truth in Lending Act (12 CFR Part 1026.32, Regulation Z). The standard for a QM excludes mortgages with loan characteristics such as negative amortization, balloon and interest-only payment schedules, terms exceeding 30 years, alt-A or no documentation, and total points and fees that exceed 3 percent of the loan amount. In addition, a QM requires that the monthly debt-to-income ratio of borrowers not exceed 43 percent. For more on the ability to repay and QM standards under Regulation Z, see the Consumer Financial Protection Bureau's website at www.consumerfinance.gov/regulations/ability-to-repay-and-qualified-mortgage-standards-under-the-truth-in-lending-act-regulation-z/.

7. The **subprime** category of residential mortgages includes loans classified by banks as subprime. This category typically includes loans made to borrowers with weakened credit histories, which may include payment delinquencies, charge-offs, judgments, or bankruptcies; reduced repayment capacity as measured by credit scores or debt-to-income ratios; or incomplete credit histories.

Measures of Supply and Demand for Commercial and Industrial Loans, by Size of Firm Seeking Loan

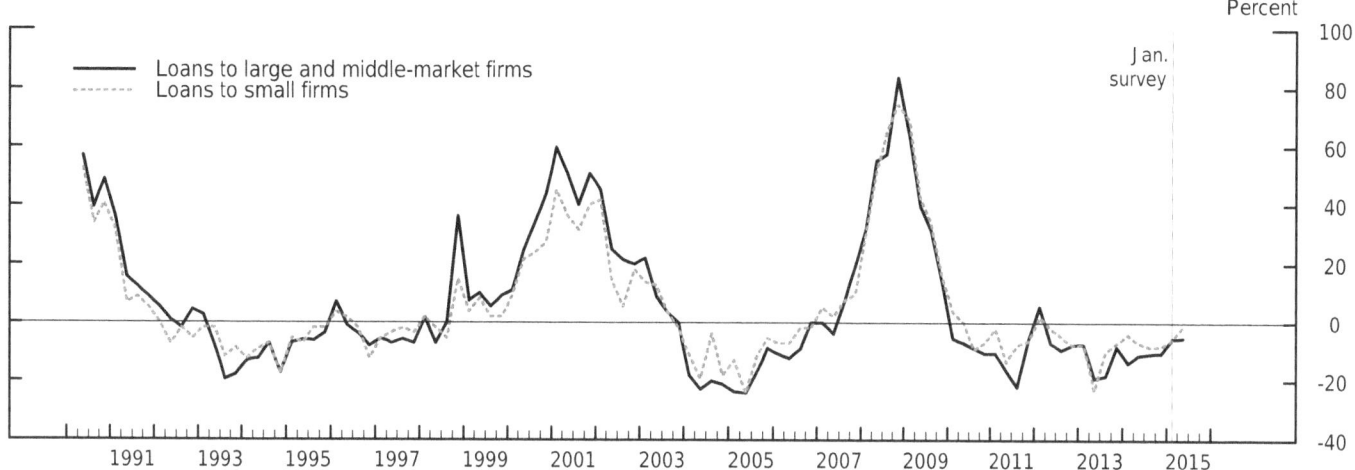

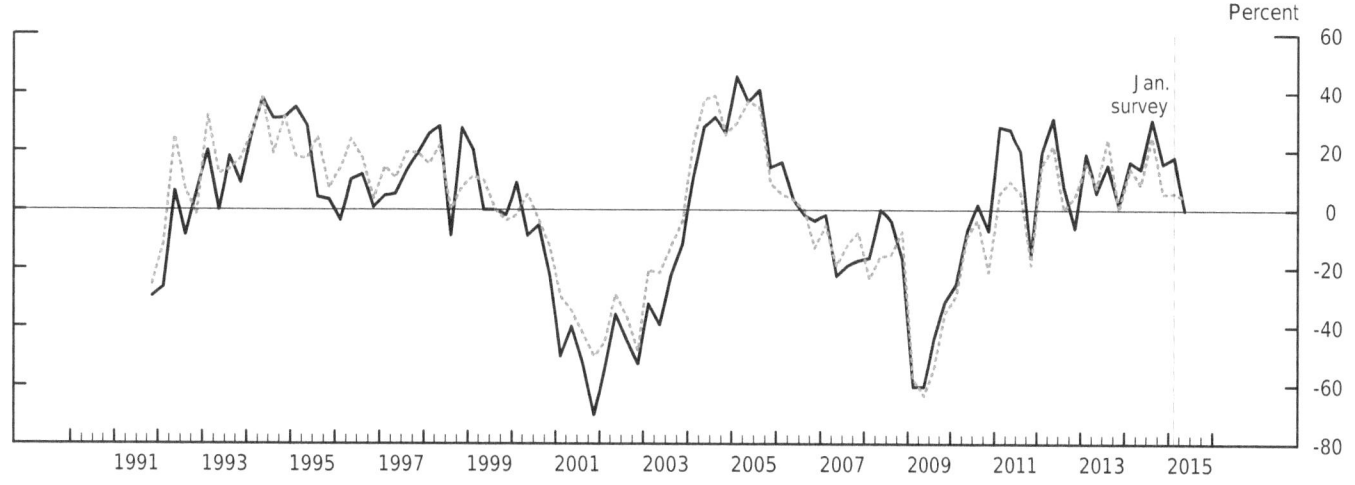

Measures of Supply and Demand for Commercial Real Estate Loans

Net Percentage of Domestic Respondents Tightening Standards for Commercial Real Estate Loans

Net Percentage of Domestic Respondents Reporting Stronger Demand for Commercial Real Estate Loans

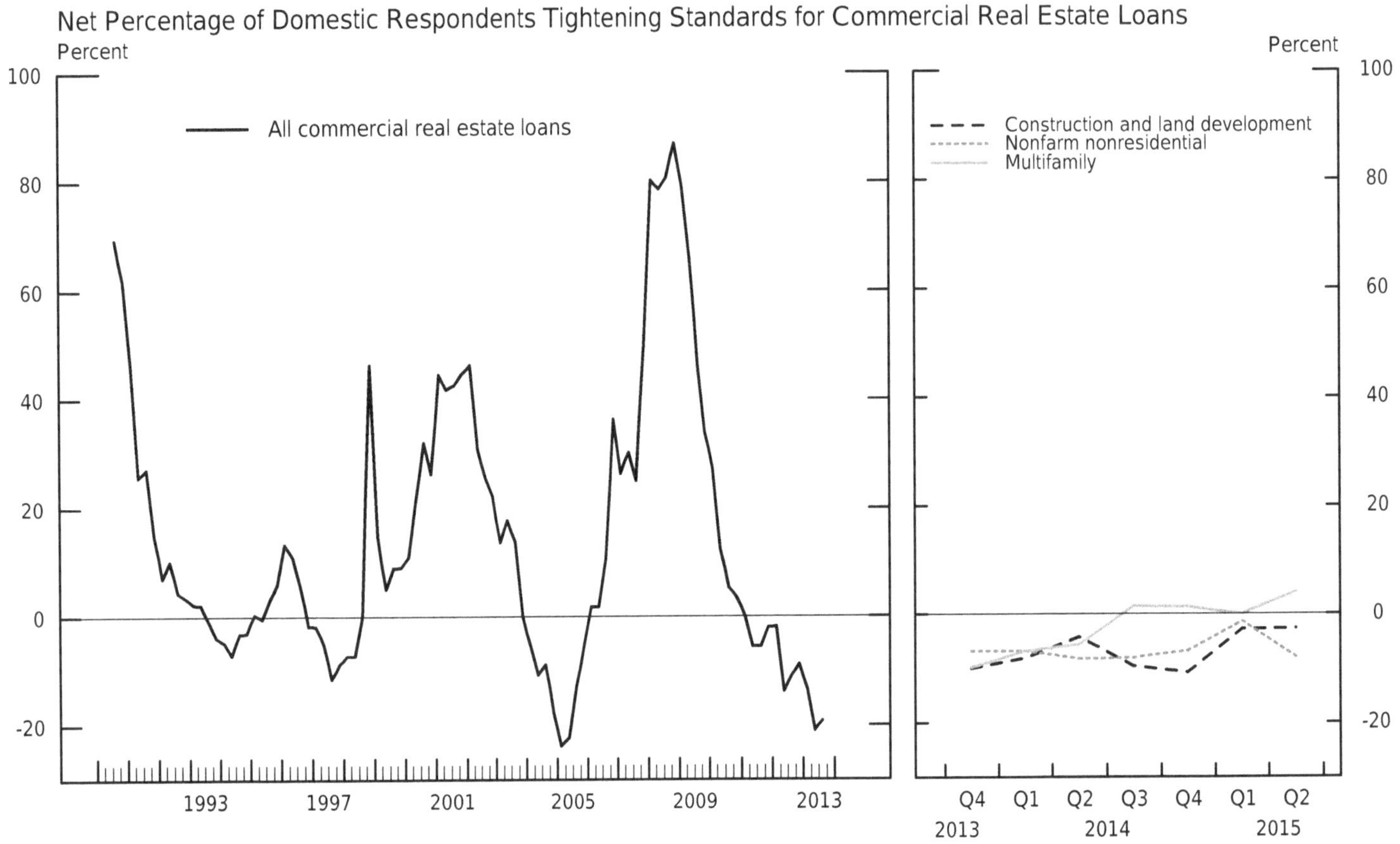

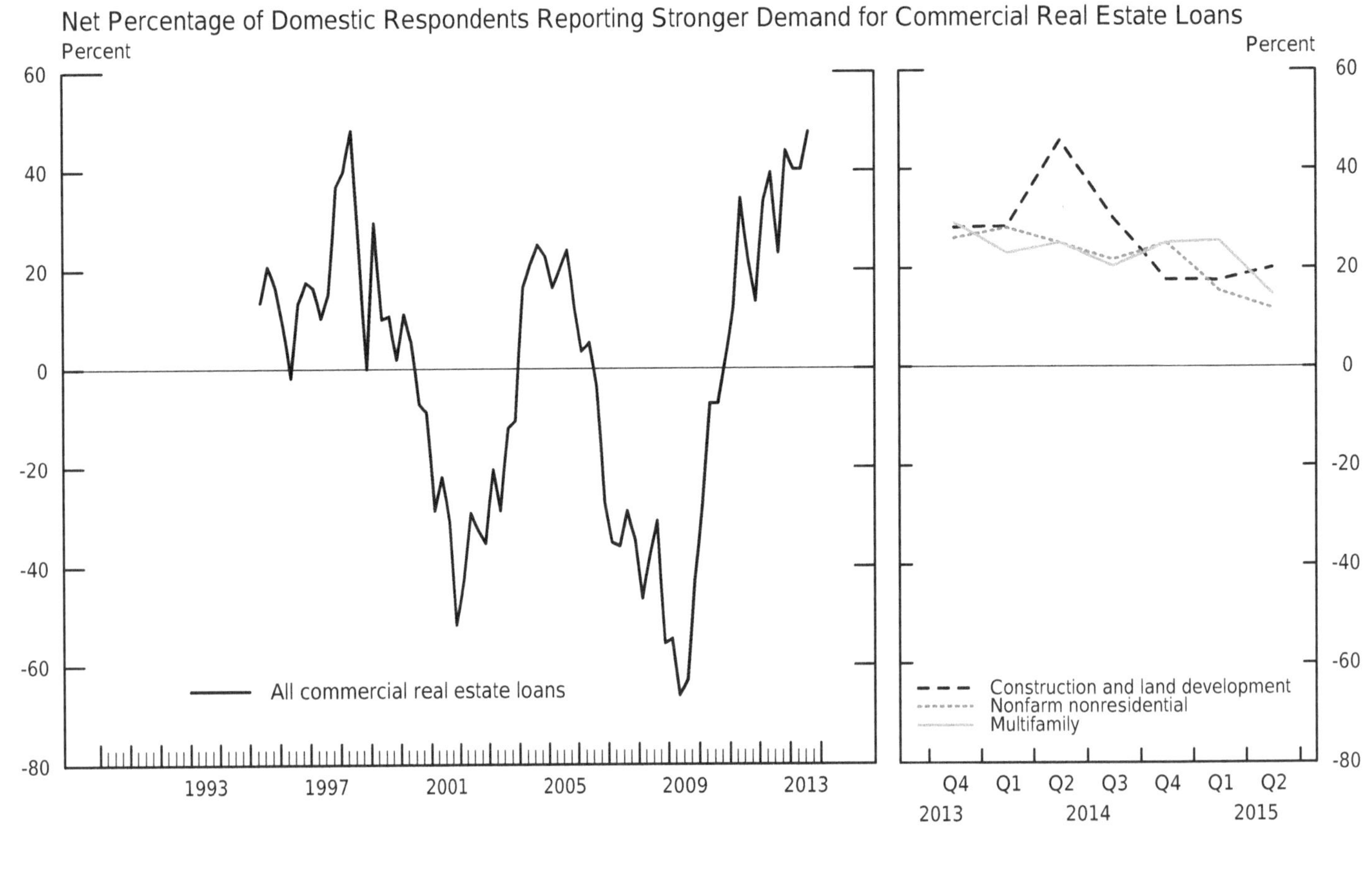

Note: For data starting in 2013:Q4, changes in demand for construction and land development, nonfarm nonresidential, and multifamily loans are reported separately.

Measures of Supply and Demand for Residential Mortgage Loans

Net Percentage of Domestic Respondents Tightening Standards for Residential Mortgage Loans

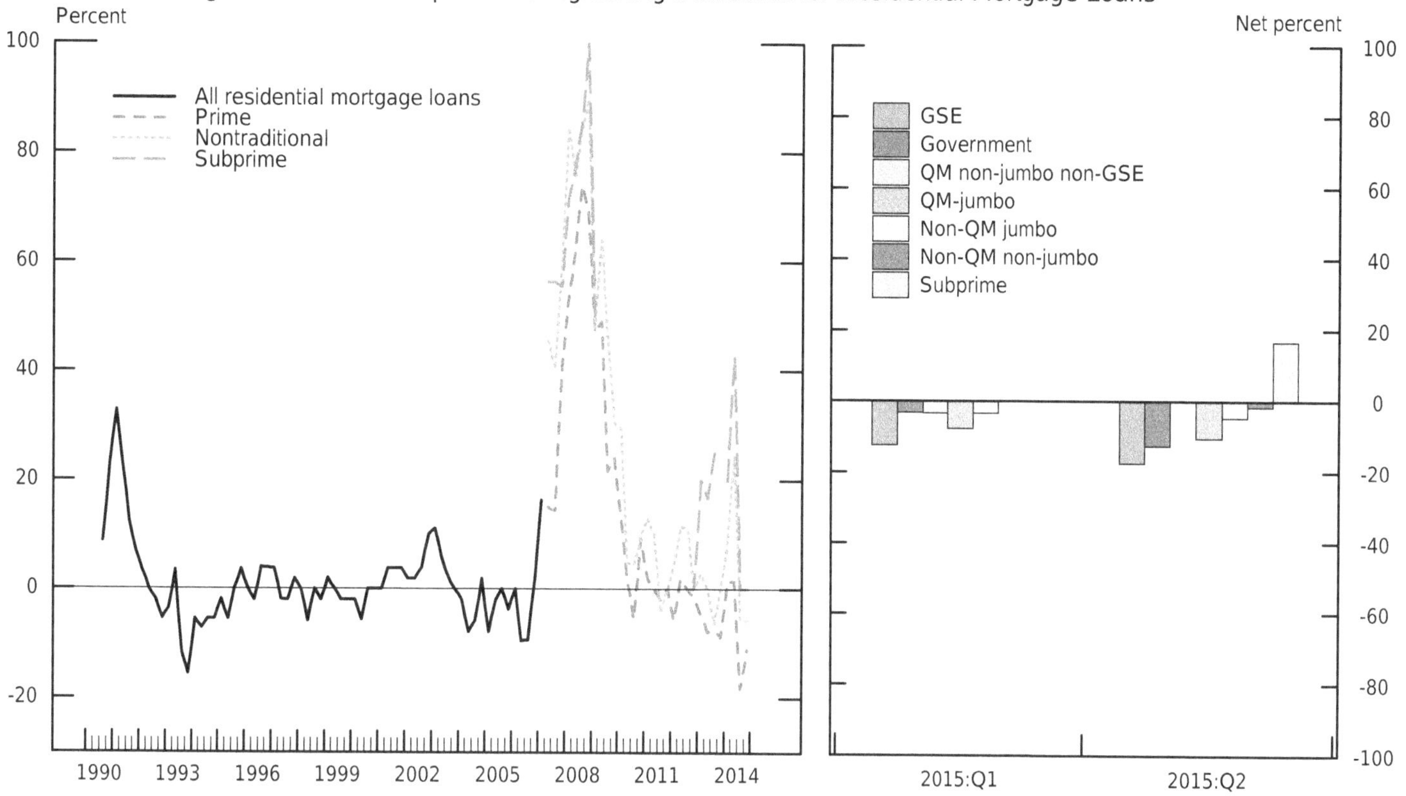

Net Percentage of Domestic Respondents Reporting Stronger Demand for Residential Mortgage Loans

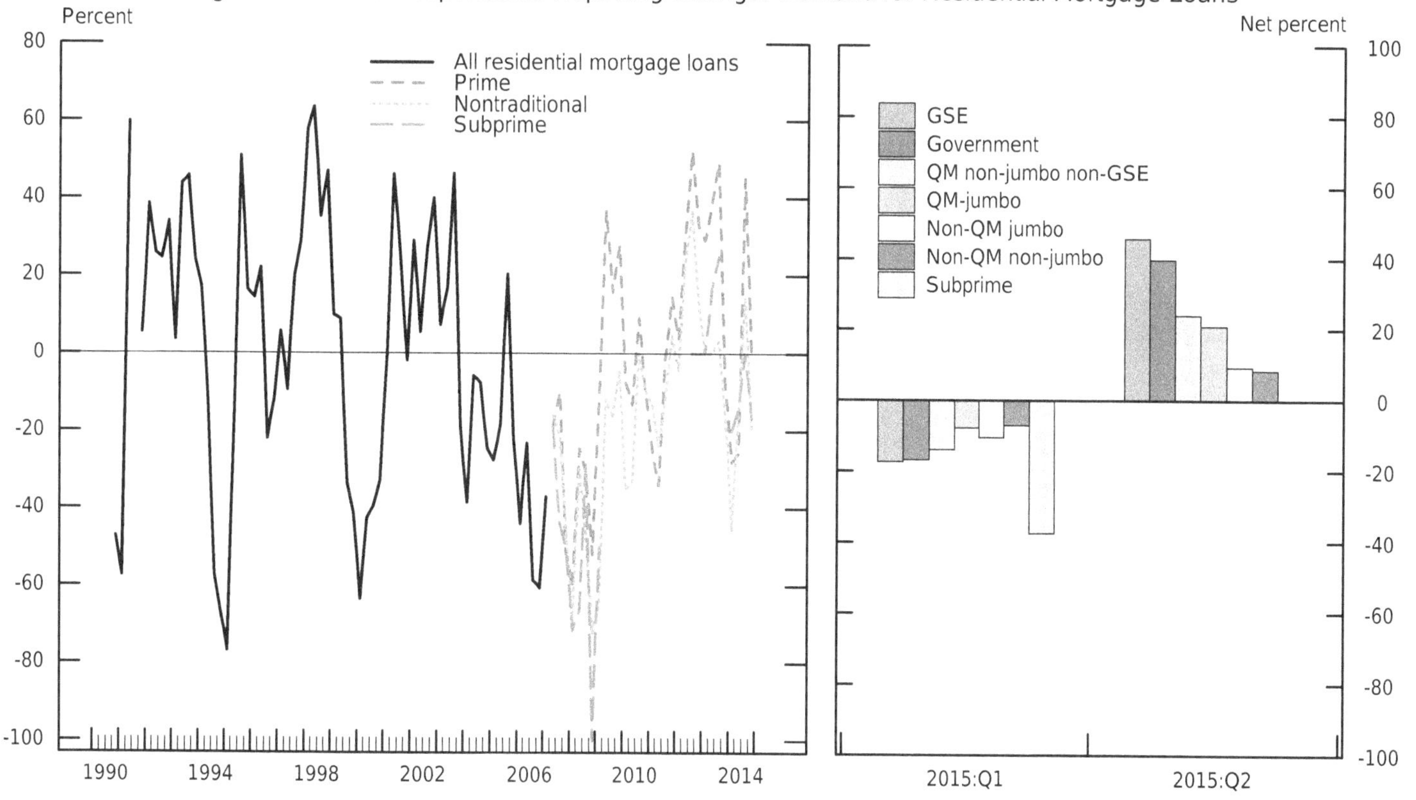

Note: For data starting in 2007:Q2, changes in standards and demand for prime, nontraditional, and subprime mortgage loans are reported separately. For data starting in 2014:Q4, changes in standards and demand were expanded into the following seven categories: GSE-eligible; government; QM non-jumbo non-GSE-eligible; QM-jumbo; non-QM jumbo; non-QM non-jumbo; and subprime. Series are not reported when the number of respondents is three or fewer.

Measures of Supply and Demand for Consumer Loans

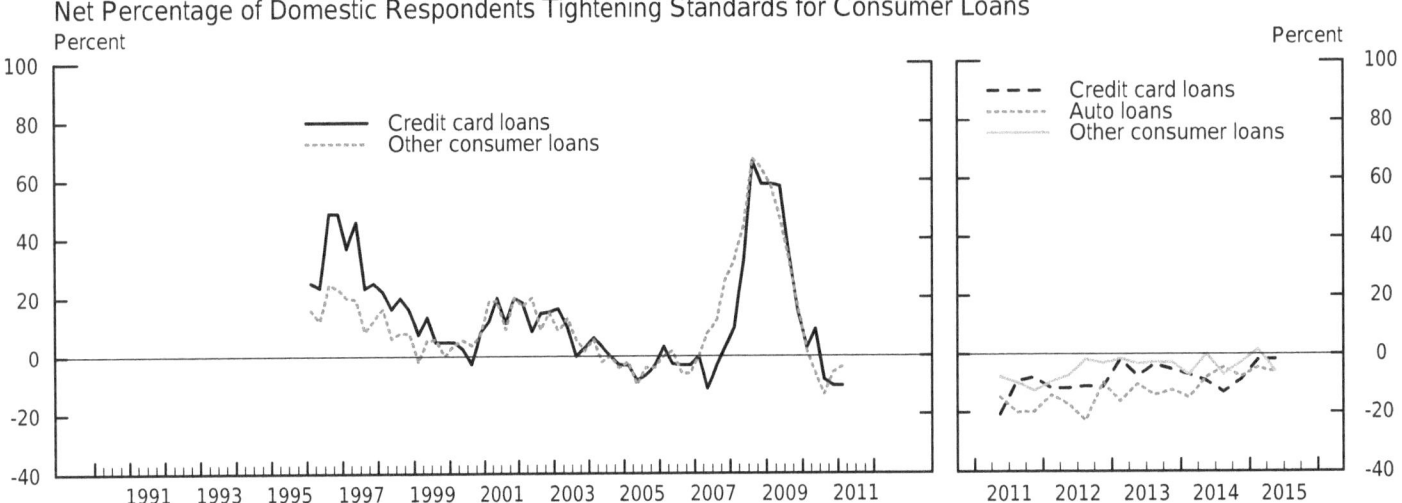

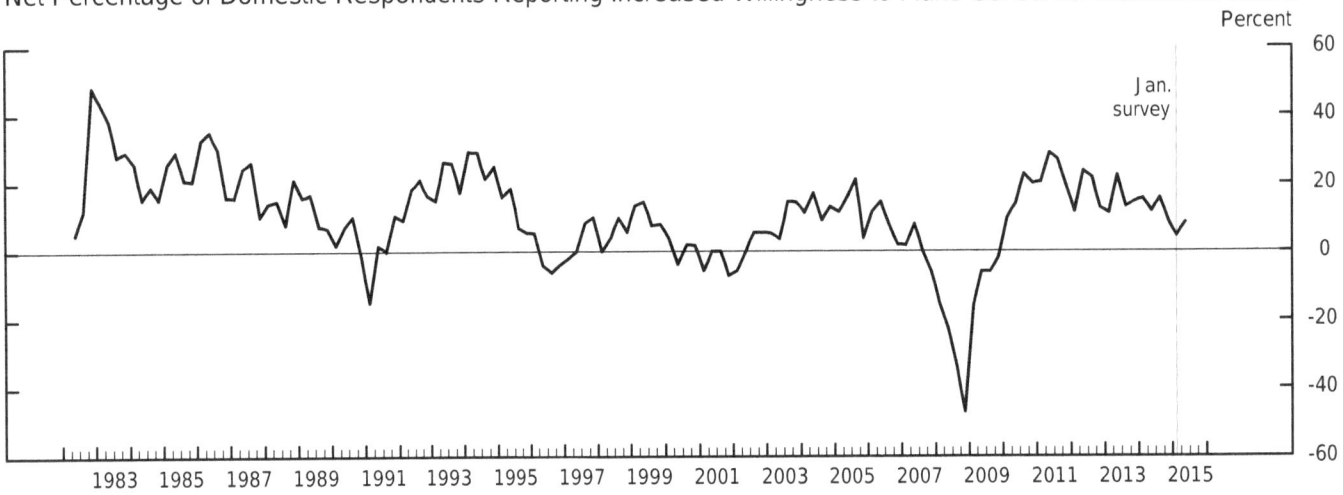

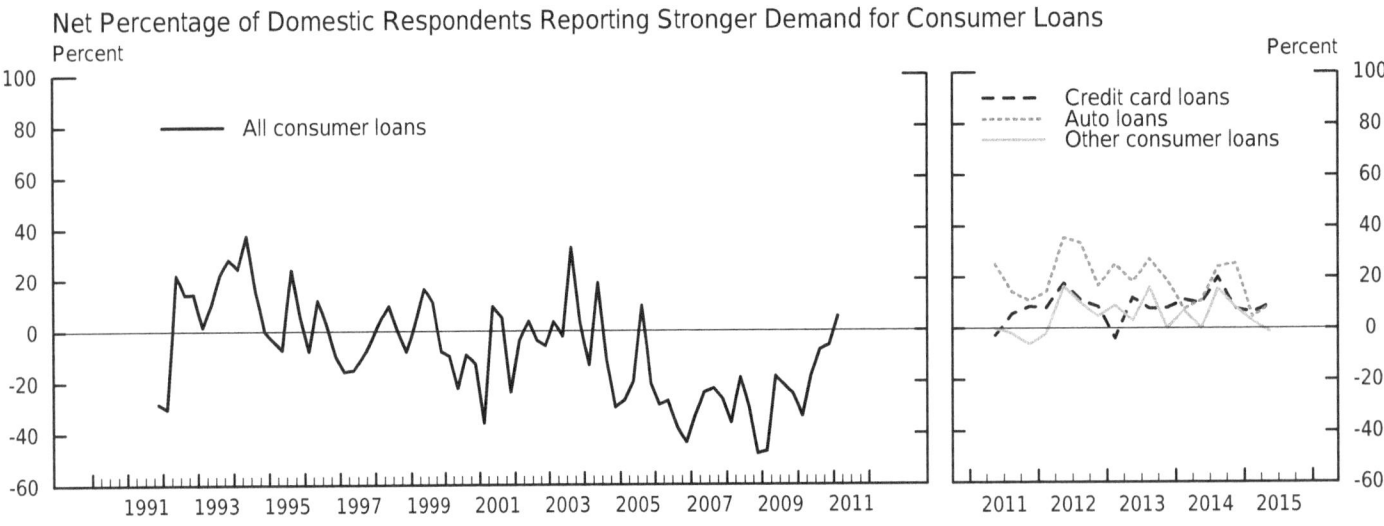

Table 1

Senior Loan Officer Opinion Survey on Bank Lending Practices at Selected Large Banks in the United States [1]

(Status of policy as of April 2015)

Questions 1-6 ask about commercial and industrial (C&I) loans at your bank. Questions 1-3 deal with changes in your bank's lending policies over the past three months. Questions 4-5 deal with changes in demand for C&I loans over the past three months. Question 6 asks about changes in prospective demand for C&I loans at your bank, as indicated by the volume of recent inquiries about the availability of new credit lines or increases in existing lines. If your bank's lending policies have not changed over the past three months, please report them as unchanged even if the policies are either restrictive or accommodative relative to longer-term norms. If your bank's policies have tightened or eased over the past three months, please so report them regardless of how they stand relative to longer-term norms. Also, please report changes in enforcement of existing policies as changes in policies.

1. Over the past three months, how have your bank's credit standards for approving applications for C&I loans or credit lines—other than those to be used to finance mergers and acquisitions—to large and middle-market firms and to small firms changed? (If your bank defines firm size differently from the categories suggested below, please use your definitions and indicate what they are.)

   A. Standards for large and middle-market firms (annual sales of $50 million or more):

	All Respondents		Large Banks		Other Banks	
	Banks	Percent	Banks	Percent	Banks	Percent
Tightened considerably	0	0.0	0	0.0	0	0.0
Tightened somewhat	3	4.0	2	4.9	1	2.9
Remained basically unchanged	65	86.7	35	85.4	30	88.2
Eased somewhat	7	9.3	4	9.8	3	8.8
Eased considerably	0	0.0	0	0.0	0	0.0
Total	75	100.0	41	100.0	34	100.0

B. Standards for small firms (annual sales of less than $50 million):

	All Respondents		Large Banks		Other Banks	
	Banks	Percent	Banks	Percent	Banks	Percent
Tightened considerably	0	0.0	0	0.0	0	0.0
Tightened somewhat	3	4.2	1	2.7	2	5.7
Remained basically unchanged	65	90.3	36	97.3	29	82.9
Eased somewhat	4	5.6	0	0.0	4	11.4
Eased considerably	0	0.0	0	0.0	0	0.0
Total	72	100.0	37	100.0	35	100.0

2. For applications for C&I loans or credit lines—other than those to be used to finance mergers and acquisitions—from large and middle-market firms and from small firms that your bank currently is willing to approve, how have the terms of those loans changed over the past three months?

A. Terms for large and middle-market firms (annual sales of $50 million or more):

a. Maximum size of credit lines

	All Respondents		Large Banks		Other Banks	
	Banks	Percent	Banks	Percent	Banks	Percent
Tightened considerably	0	0.0	0	0.0	0	0.0
Tightened somewhat	2	2.7	0	0.0	2	5.9
Remained basically unchanged	61	81.3	31	75.6	30	88.2
Eased somewhat	12	16.0	10	24.4	2	5.9
Eased considerably	0	0.0	0	0.0	0	0.0
Total	75	100.0	41	100.0	34	100.0

b. Maximum maturity of loans or credit lines

	All Respondents		Large Banks		Other Banks	
	Banks	Percent	Banks	Percent	Banks	Percent
Tightened considerably	0	0.0	0	0.0	0	0.0
Tightened somewhat	0	0.0	0	0.0	0	0.0
Remained basically unchanged	74	98.7	41	100.0	33	97.1
Eased somewhat	1	1.3	0	0.0	1	2.9
Eased considerably	0	0.0	0	0.0	0	0.0
Total	75	100.0	41	100.0	34	100.0

c. Costs of credit lines

	All Respondents		Large Banks		Other Banks	
	Banks	Percent	Banks	Percent	Banks	Percent
Tightened considerably	0	0.0	0	0.0	0	0.0
Tightened somewhat	1	1.3	1	2.4	0	0.0
Remained basically unchanged	53	70.7	29	70.7	24	70.6
Eased somewhat	20	26.7	11	26.8	9	26.5
Eased considerably	1	1.3	0	0.0	1	2.9
Total	75	100.0	41	100.0	34	100.0

d. Spreads of loan rates over your bank's cost of funds (wider spreads=tightened, narrower spreads=eased)

	All Respondents		Large Banks		Other Banks	
	Banks	Percent	Banks	Percent	Banks	Percent
Tightened considerably	0	0.0	0	0.0	0	0.0
Tightened somewhat	3	4.0	3	7.3	0	0.0
Remained basically unchanged	39	52.0	21	51.2	18	52.9
Eased somewhat	31	41.3	17	41.5	14	41.2
Eased considerably	2	2.7	0	0.0	2	5.9
Total	75	100.0	41	100.0	34	100.0

e. Premiums charged on riskier loans

	All Respondents		Large Banks		Other Banks	
	Banks	Percent	Banks	Percent	Banks	Percent
Tightened considerably	0	0.0	0	0.0	0	0.0
Tightened somewhat	3	4.0	3	7.3	0	0.0
Remained basically unchanged	62	82.7	31	75.6	31	91.2
Eased somewhat	10	13.3	7	17.1	3	8.8
Eased considerably	0	0.0	0	0.0	0	0.0
Total	75	100.0	41	100.0	34	100.0

f. Loan covenants

	All Respondents		Large Banks		Other Banks	
	Banks	Percent	Banks	Percent	Banks	Percent
Tightened considerably	0	0.0	0	0.0	0	0.0
Tightened somewhat	4	5.3	3	7.3	1	2.9
Remained basically unchanged	61	81.3	32	78.0	29	85.3
Eased somewhat	10	13.3	6	14.6	4	11.8
Eased considerably	0	0.0	0	0.0	0	0.0
Total	75	100.0	41	100.0	34	100.0

g. Collateralization requirements

	All Respondents		Large Banks		Other Banks	
	Banks	Percent	Banks	Percent	Banks	Percent
Tightened considerably	0	0.0	0	0.0	0	0.0
Tightened somewhat	0	0.0	0	0.0	0	0.0
Remained basically unchanged	71	94.7	39	95.1	32	94.1
Eased somewhat	4	5.3	2	4.9	2	5.9
Eased considerably	0	0.0	0	0.0	0	0.0
Total	75	100.0	41	100.0	34	100.0

h. Use of interest rate floors (more use=tightened, less use=eased)

	All Respondents		Large Banks		Other Banks	
	Banks	Percent	Banks	Percent	Banks	Percent
Tightened considerably	0	0.0	0	0.0	0	0.0
Tightened somewhat	2	2.8	0	0.0	2	6.3
Remained basically unchanged	54	76.1	33	84.6	21	65.6
Eased somewhat	12	16.9	4	10.3	8	25.0
Eased considerably	3	4.2	2	5.1	1	3.1
Total	71	100.0	39	100.0	32	100.0

B. Terms for small firms (annual sales of less than $50 million):

a. Maximum size of credit lines

	All Respondents		Large Banks		Other Banks	
	Banks	Percent	Banks	Percent	Banks	Percent
Tightened considerably	0	0.0	0	0.0	0	0.0
Tightened somewhat	0	0.0	0	0.0	0	0.0
Remained basically unchanged	69	97.2	35	94.6	34	100.0
Eased somewhat	2	2.8	2	5.4	0	0.0
Eased considerably	0	0.0	0	0.0	0	0.0
Total	71	100.0	37	100.0	34	100.0

b. Maximum maturity of loans or credit lines

	All Respondents		Large Banks		Other Banks	
	Banks	Percent	Banks	Percent	Banks	Percent
Tightened considerably	0	0.0	0	0.0	0	0.0
Tightened somewhat	0	0.0	0	0.0	0	0.0
Remained basically unchanged	68	95.8	36	97.3	32	94.1
Eased somewhat	3	4.2	1	2.7	2	5.9
Eased considerably	0	0.0	0	0.0	0	0.0
Total	71	100.0	37	100.0	34	100.0

c. Costs of credit lines

	All Respondents		Large Banks		Other Banks	
	Banks	Percent	Banks	Percent	Banks	Percent
Tightened considerably	0	0.0	0	0.0	0	0.0
Tightened somewhat	0	0.0	0	0.0	0	0.0
Remained basically unchanged	56	78.9	30	81.1	26	76.5
Eased somewhat	15	21.1	7	18.9	8	23.5
Eased considerably	0	0.0	0	0.0	0	0.0
Total	71	100.0	37	100.0	34	100.0

d. Spreads of loan rates over your bank's cost of funds (wider spreads=tightened, narrower spreads=eased)

	All Respondents		Large Banks		Other Banks	
	Banks	Percent	Banks	Percent	Banks	Percent
Tightened considerably	0	0.0	0	0.0	0	0.0
Tightened somewhat	2	2.8	2	5.4	0	0.0
Remained basically unchanged	39	54.9	23	62.2	16	47.1
Eased somewhat	29	40.8	12	32.4	17	50.0
Eased considerably	1	1.4	0	0.0	1	2.9
Total	71	100.0	37	100.0	34	100.0

e. Premiums charged on riskier loans

	All Respondents		Large Banks		Other Banks	
	Banks	Percent	Banks	Percent	Banks	Percent
Tightened considerably	0	0.0	0	0.0	0	0.0
Tightened somewhat	2	2.8	2	5.4	0	0.0
Remained basically unchanged	64	90.1	32	86.5	32	94.1
Eased somewhat	5	7.0	3	8.1	2	5.9
Eased considerably	0	0.0	0	0.0	0	0.0
Total	71	100.0	37	100.0	34	100.0

f. Loan covenants

	All Respondents		Large Banks		Other Banks	
	Banks	Percent	Banks	Percent	Banks	Percent
Tightened considerably	0	0.0	0	0.0	0	0.0
Tightened somewhat	2	2.8	1	2.7	1	2.9
Remained basically unchanged	61	85.9	33	89.2	28	82.4
Eased somewhat	8	11.3	3	8.1	5	14.7
Eased considerably	0	0.0	0	0.0	0	0.0
Total	71	100.0	37	100.0	34	100.0

g. Collateralization requirements

	All Respondents		Large Banks		Other Banks	
	Banks	Percent	Banks	Percent	Banks	Percent
Tightened considerably	0	0.0	0	0.0	0	0.0
Tightened somewhat	0	0.0	0	0.0	0	0.0
Remained basically unchanged	69	97.2	37	100.0	32	94.1
Eased somewhat	2	2.8	0	0.0	2	5.9
Eased considerably	0	0.0	0	0.0	0	0.0
Total	71	100.0	37	100.0	34	100.0

h. Use of interest rate floors (more use=tightened, less use=eased)

	All Respondents		Large Banks		Other Banks	
	Banks	Percent	Banks	Percent	Banks	Percent
Tightened considerably	0	0.0	0	0.0	0	0.0
Tightened somewhat	2	2.9	0	0.0	2	6.1
Remained basically unchanged	53	77.9	32	91.4	21	63.6
Eased somewhat	11	16.2	2	5.7	9	27.3
Eased considerably	2	2.9	1	2.9	1	3.0
Total	68	100.0	35	100.0	33	100.0

3. If your bank has tightened or eased its credit standards or its terms for C&I loans or credit lines over the past three months (as described in questions 1 and 2), how important have been the following possible reasons for the change?

A. Possible reasons for tightening credit standards or loan terms:

a. Deterioration in your bank's current or expected capital position

	All Respondents		Large Banks		Other Banks	
	Banks	Percent	Banks	Percent	Banks	Percent
Not important	11	91.7	6	85.7	5	100.0
Somewhat important	1	8.3	1	14.3	0	0.0
Very important	0	0.0	0	0.0	0	0.0
Total	12	100.0	7	100.0	5	100.0

b. Less favorable or more uncertain economic outlook

	All Respondents		Large Banks		Other Banks	
	Banks	Percent	Banks	Percent	Banks	Percent
Not important	5	41.7	3	42.9	2	40.0
Somewhat important	7	58.3	4	57.1	3	60.0
Very important	0	0.0	0	0.0	0	0.0
Total	12	100.0	7	100.0	5	100.0

c. Worsening of industry-specific problems (please specify industries)

	All Respondents		Large Banks		Other Banks	
	Banks	Percent	Banks	Percent	Banks	Percent
Not important	4	33.3	2	28.6	2	40.0
Somewhat important	6	50.0	5	71.4	1	20.0
Very important	2	16.7	0	0.0	2	40.0
Total	12	100.0	7	100.0	5	100.0

d. Less aggressive competition from other banks or nonbank lenders (other financial intermediaries or the capital markets)

	All Respondents		Large Banks		Other Banks	
	Banks	Percent	Banks	Percent	Banks	Percent
Not important	10	83.3	6	85.7	4	80.0
Somewhat important	2	16.7	1	14.3	1	20.0
Very important	0	0.0	0	0.0	0	0.0
Total	12	100.0	7	100.0	5	100.0

e. Reduced tolerance for risk

	All Respondents		Large Banks		Other Banks	
	Banks	Percent	Banks	Percent	Banks	Percent
Not important	8	66.7	5	71.4	3	60.0
Somewhat important	3	25.0	2	28.6	1	20.0
Very important	1	8.3	0	0.0	1	20.0
Total	12	100.0	7	100.0	5	100.0

f. Decreased liquidity in the secondary market for these loans

	All Respondents		Large Banks		Other Banks	
	Banks	Percent	Banks	Percent	Banks	Percent
Not important	9	75.0	4	57.1	5	100.0
Somewhat important	3	25.0	3	42.9	0	0.0
Very important	0	0.0	0	0.0	0	0.0
Total	12	100.0	7	100.0	5	100.0

g. Deterioration in your bank's current or expected liquidity position

	All Respondents		Large Banks		Other Banks	
	Banks	Percent	Banks	Percent	Banks	Percent
Not important	12	100.0	7	100.0	5	100.0
Somewhat important	0	0.0	0	0.0	0	0.0
Very important	0	0.0	0	0.0	0	0.0
Total	12	100.0	7	100.0	5	100.0

h. Increased concerns about the effects of legislative changes, supervisory actions, or changes in accounting standards

	All Respondents		Large Banks		Other Banks	
	Banks	Percent	Banks	Percent	Banks	Percent
Not important	5	41.7	3	42.9	2	40.0
Somewhat important	4	33.3	3	42.9	1	20.0
Very important	3	25.0	1	14.3	2	40.0
Total	12	100.0	7	100.0	5	100.0

B. Possible reasons for easing credit standards or loan terms:

a. Improvement in your bank's current or expected capital position

	All Respondents		Large Banks		Other Banks	
	Banks	Percent	Banks	Percent	Banks	Percent
Not important	37	86.0	22	91.7	15	78.9
Somewhat important	4	9.3	2	8.3	2	10.5
Very important	2	4.7	0	0.0	2	10.5
Total	43	100.0	24	100.0	19	100.0

b. More favorable or less uncertain economic outlook

	All Respondents		Large Banks		Other Banks	
	Banks	Percent	Banks	Percent	Banks	Percent
Not important	27	62.8	16	66.7	11	57.9
Somewhat important	11	25.6	7	29.2	4	21.1
Very important	5	11.6	1	4.2	4	21.1
Total	43	100.0	24	100.0	19	100.0

c. Improvement in industry-specific problems (please specify industries)

	All Respondents		Large Banks		Other Banks	
	Banks	Percent	Banks	Percent	Banks	Percent
Not important	31	72.1	21	87.5	10	52.6
Somewhat important	10	23.3	3	12.5	7	36.8
Very important	2	4.7	0	0.0	2	10.5
Total	43	100.0	24	100.0	19	100.0

d. More aggressive competition from other banks or nonbank lenders (other financial intermediaries or the capital markets)

	All Respondents		Large Banks		Other Banks	
	Banks	Percent	Banks	Percent	Banks	Percent
Not important	3	7.0	1	4.2	2	10.5
Somewhat important	13	30.2	7	29.2	6	31.6
Very important	27	62.8	16	66.7	11	57.9
Total	43	100.0	24	100.0	19	100.0

e. Increased tolerance for risk

	All Respondents		Large Banks		Other Banks	
	Banks	Percent	Banks	Percent	Banks	Percent
Not important	28	65.1	18	75.0	10	52.6
Somewhat important	12	27.9	4	16.7	8	42.1
Very important	3	7.0	2	8.3	1	5.3
Total	43	100.0	24	100.0	19	100.0

f. Increased liquidity in the secondary market for these loans

	All Respondents		Large Banks		Other Banks	
	Banks	Percent	Banks	Percent	Banks	Percent
Not important	34	79.1	20	83.3	14	73.7
Somewhat important	8	18.6	4	16.7	4	21.1
Very important	1	2.3	0	0.0	1	5.3
Total	43	100.0	24	100.0	19	100.0

g. Improvement in your bank's current or expected liquidity position

	All Respondents		Large Banks		Other Banks	
	Banks	Percent	Banks	Percent	Banks	Percent
Not important	36	83.7	22	91.7	14	73.7
Somewhat important	6	14.0	2	8.3	4	21.1
Very important	1	2.3	0	0.0	1	5.3
Total	43	100.0	24	100.0	19	100.0

h. Reduced concerns about the effects of legislative changes, supervisory actions, or changes in accounting standards

	All Respondents		Large Banks		Other Banks	
	Banks	Percent	Banks	Percent	Banks	Percent
Not important	35	81.4	22	91.7	13	68.4
Somewhat important	7	16.3	2	8.3	5	26.3
Very important	1	2.3	0	0.0	1	5.3
Total	43	100.0	24	100.0	19	100.0

4. Apart from normal seasonal variation, how has demand for C&I loans changed over the past three months? (Please consider only funds actually disbursed as opposed to requests for new or increased lines of credit.)

   A. Demand for C&I loans from large and middle-market firms (annual sales of $50 million or more):

	All Respondents		Large Banks		Other Banks	
	Banks	Percent	Banks	Percent	Banks	Percent
Substantially stronger	0	0.0	0	0.0	0	0.0
Moderately stronger	12	16.0	4	9.8	8	23.5
About the same	51	68.0	29	70.7	22	64.7
Moderately weaker	12	16.0	8	19.5	4	11.8
Substantially weaker	0	0.0	0	0.0	0	0.0
Total	75	100.0	41	100.0	34	100.0

   B. Demand for C&I loans from small firms (annual sales of less than $50 million):

	All Respondents		Large Banks		Other Banks	
	Banks	Percent	Banks	Percent	Banks	Percent
Substantially stronger	0	0.0	0	0.0	0	0.0
Moderately stronger	11	15.1	2	5.3	9	25.7
About the same	54	74.0	32	84.2	22	62.9
Moderately weaker	8	11.0	4	10.5	4	11.4
Substantially weaker	0	0.0	0	0.0	0	0.0
Total	73	100.0	38	100.0	35	100.0

5. If demand for C&I loans has strengthened or weakened over the past three months (as described in question 4), how important have been the following possible reasons for the change?

   A. If stronger loan demand (answer 1 or 2 to question 4A or 4B), possible reasons:

   a. Customer inventory financing needs increased

	All Respondents		Large Banks		Other Banks	
	Banks	Percent	Banks	Percent	Banks	Percent
Not important	6	42.9	4	80.0	2	22.2
Somewhat important	8	57.1	1	20.0	7	77.8
Very important	0	0.0	0	0.0	0	0.0
Total	14	100.0	5	100.0	9	100.0

   b. Customer accounts receivable financing needs increased

	All Respondents		Large Banks		Other Banks	
	Banks	Percent	Banks	Percent	Banks	Percent
Not important	5	35.7	4	80.0	1	11.1
Somewhat important	9	64.3	1	20.0	8	88.9
Very important	0	0.0	0	0.0	0	0.0
Total	14	100.0	5	100.0	9	100.0

   c. Customer investment in plant or equipment increased

	All Respondents		Large Banks		Other Banks	
	Banks	Percent	Banks	Percent	Banks	Percent
Not important	5	35.7	2	40.0	3	33.3
Somewhat important	9	64.3	3	60.0	6	66.7
Very important	0	0.0	0	0.0	0	0.0
Total	14	100.0	5	100.0	9	100.0

d. Customer internally generated funds decreased

	All Respondents		Large Banks		Other Banks	
	Banks	Percent	Banks	Percent	Banks	Percent
Not important	12	85.7	5	100.0	7	77.8
Somewhat important	1	7.1	0	0.0	1	11.1
Very important	1	7.1	0	0.0	1	11.1
Total	14	100.0	5	100.0	9	100.0

e. Customer merger or acquisition financing needs increased

	All Respondents		Large Banks		Other Banks	
	Banks	Percent	Banks	Percent	Banks	Percent
Not important	6	42.9	1	20.0	5	55.6
Somewhat important	5	35.7	1	20.0	4	44.4
Very important	3	21.4	3	60.0	0	0.0
Total	14	100.0	5	100.0	9	100.0

f. Customer borrowing shifted to your bank from other bank or nonbank sources because these other sources became less attractive

	All Respondents		Large Banks		Other Banks	
	Banks	Percent	Banks	Percent	Banks	Percent
Not important	6	42.9	2	40.0	4	44.4
Somewhat important	6	42.9	2	40.0	4	44.4
Very important	2	14.3	1	20.0	1	11.1
Total	14	100.0	5	100.0	9	100.0

g. Customers' precautionary demand for cash and liquidity increased

	All Respondents		Large Banks		Other Banks	
	Banks	Percent	Banks	Percent	Banks	Percent
Not important	13	92.9	5	100.0	8	88.9
Somewhat important	1	7.1	0	0.0	1	11.1
Very important	0	0.0	0	0.0	0	0.0
Total	14	100.0	5	100.0	9	100.0

B. If weaker loan demand (answer 4 or 5 to question 4A or 4B), possible reasons:

a. Customer inventory financing needs decreased

	All Respondents		Large Banks		Other Banks	
	Banks	Percent	Banks	Percent	Banks	Percent
Not important	12	85.7	8	88.9	4	80.0
Somewhat important	2	14.3	1	11.1	1	20.0
Very important	0	0.0	0	0.0	0	0.0
Total	14	100.0	9	100.0	5	100.0

b. Customer accounts receivable financing needs decreased

	All Respondents		Large Banks		Other Banks	
	Banks	Percent	Banks	Percent	Banks	Percent
Not important	13	92.9	9	100.0	4	80.0
Somewhat important	1	7.1	0	0.0	1	20.0
Very important	0	0.0	0	0.0	0	0.0
Total	14	100.0	9	100.0	5	100.0

c. Customer investment in plant or equipment decreased

	All Respondents		Large Banks		Other Banks	
	Banks	Percent	Banks	Percent	Banks	Percent
Not important	9	64.3	8	88.9	1	20.0
Somewhat important	4	28.6	1	11.1	3	60.0
Very important	1	7.1	0	0.0	1	20.0
Total	14	100.0	9	100.0	5	100.0

d. Customer internally generated funds increased

	All Respondents		Large Banks		Other Banks	
	Banks	Percent	Banks	Percent	Banks	Percent
Not important	10	71.4	8	88.9	2	40.0
Somewhat important	3	21.4	0	0.0	3	60.0
Very important	1	7.1	1	11.1	0	0.0
Total	14	100.0	9	100.0	5	100.0

e. Customer merger or acquisition financing needs decreased

	All Respondents		Large Banks		Other Banks	
	Banks	Percent	Banks	Percent	Banks	Percent
Not important	6	42.9	5	55.6	1	20.0
Somewhat important	7	50.0	3	33.3	4	80.0
Very important	1	7.1	1	11.1	0	0.0
Total	14	100.0	9	100.0	5	100.0

f. Customer borrowing shifted from your bank to other bank or nonbank sources because these other sources became more attractive

	All Respondents		Large Banks		Other Banks	
	Banks	Percent	Banks	Percent	Banks	Percent
Not important	7	50.0	4	44.4	3	60.0
Somewhat important	6	42.9	4	44.4	2	40.0
Very important	1	7.1	1	11.1	0	0.0
Total	14	100.0	9	100.0	5	100.0

g. Customers' precautionary demand for cash and liquidity decreased

	All Respondents		Large Banks		Other Banks	
	Banks	Percent	Banks	Percent	Banks	Percent
Not important	14	100.0	9	100.0	5	100.0
Somewhat important	0	0.0	0	0.0	0	0.0
Very important	0	0.0	0	0.0	0	0.0
Total	14	100.0	9	100.0	5	100.0

6. At your bank, apart from seasonal variation, how has the number of inquiries from potential business borrowers regarding the availability and terms of new credit lines or increases in existing lines changed over the past three months? (Please consider only inquiries for additional or increased C&I lines as opposed to the refinancing of existing loans.)

	All Respondents		Large Banks		Other Banks	
	Banks	Percent	Banks	Percent	Banks	Percent
The number of inquiries has increased substantially	0	0.0	0	0.0	0	0.0
The number of inquiries has increased moderately	11	14.5	3	7.3	8	22.9
The number of inquiries has stayed about the same	56	73.7	32	78.0	24	68.6
The number of inquiries has decreased moderately	9	11.8	6	14.6	3	8.6
The number of inquiries has decreased substantially	0	0.0	0	0.0	0	0.0
Total	76	100.0	41	100.0	35	100.0

Recent declines in oil prices may have led to strains in firms involved in oil and natural gas drilling/extraction and in the companies that provide support to those firms. Question 7 asks you to indicate what fraction of C&I loans held on your books are made to firms in the oil and natural gas drilling/extraction sector. Question 8 asks about your outlook for delinquencies and charge-offs on such loans. Question 9 asks about changes in credit policies made by your bank in response to developments in the oil and natural gas drilling/extraction sector.

7. Approximately what fraction of C&I loans currently outstanding on your bank's books were made to firms in the oil and natural gas drilling/extraction sector?

	All Respondents		**Large Banks**		**Other Banks**	
	Banks	Percent	Banks	Percent	Banks	Percent
More than 30 percent	0	0.0	0	0.0	0	0.0
More than 20 but less than 30 percent	2	3.9	2	6.1	0	0.0
More than 10 but less than 20 percent	7	13.7	5	15.2	2	11.1
Less than 10 percent	42	82.4	26	78.8	16	88.9
Total	51	100.0	33	100.0	18	100.0

For this question, 23 respondents answered "My bank does not make loans or extend lines of credit to firms in the oil and natural gas drilling/extraction sector."

8. Assuming that economic activity progresses in line with consensus forecasts, and energy commodity prices evolve in line with current future prices, what is your outlook for delinquencies and charge- offs on your bank's loans to firms in the oil and natural gas drilling/extraction sector over the remainder of 2015?

	All Respondents		Large Banks		Other Banks	
	Banks	Percent	Banks	Percent	Banks	Percent
Loan quality is likely to improve substantially	0	0.0	0	0.0	0	0.0
Loan quality is likely to improve somewhat	1	2.0	0	0.0	1	5.6
Loan quality is likely to remain around current levels	20	39.2	14	42.4	6	33.3
Loan quality is likely to deteriorate somewhat	30	58.8	19	57.6	11	61.1
Loan quality is likely to deteriorate substantially	0	0.0	0	0.0	0	0.0
Total	51	100.0	33	100.0	18	100.0

For this question, 21 respondents answered "My bank does not hold loans to firms in the oil and natural gas drilling/extraction sector."

9. Please indicate how important each of the following actions are in your bank's efforts to mitigate risks of loan losses from loans made to firms in the oil and natural gas drilling/extraction sector. (Please rate *each* possible action using the following scale: 1=not important, 2=somewhat important, 3=very important).

a. Tightening underwriting policies on new loans or lines of credit made to firms in this sector

	All Respondents		Large Banks		Other Banks	
	Banks	Percent	Banks	Percent	Banks	Percent
Not important	15	29.4	9	27.3	6	33.3
Somewhat important	21	41.2	15	45.5	6	33.3
Very important	15	29.4	9	27.3	6	33.3
Total	51	100.0	33	100.0	18	100.0

b. Enforcing material adverse change clauses or other convenants to limit draws on existing credit lines to firms in this sector

	All Respondents		Large Banks		Other Banks	
	Banks	Percent	Banks	Percent	Banks	Percent
Not important	26	51.0	16	48.5	10	55.6
Somewhat important	20	39.2	13	39.4	7	38.9
Very important	5	9.8	4	12.1	1	5.6
Total	51	100.0	33	100.0	18	100.0

c. Reducing the size of existing credit lines to firms in this sector

	All Respondents		Large Banks		Other Banks	
	Banks	Percent	Banks	Percent	Banks	Percent
Not important	10	19.6	3	9.1	7	38.9
Somewhat important	28	54.9	18	54.5	10	55.6
Very important	13	25.5	12	36.4	1	5.6
Total	51	100.0	33	100.0	18	100.0

d. Restructuring outstanding loans to make them more robust to the revised outlook for energy prices

	All Respondents		Large Banks		Other Banks	
	Banks	Percent	Banks	Percent	Banks	Percent
Not important	9	17.6	4	12.1	5	27.8
Somewhat important	27	52.9	18	54.5	9	50.0
Very important	15	29.4	11	33.3	4	22.2
Total	51	100.0	33	100.0	18	100.0

e. Requiring additional collateral to better secure loans or credit lines to firms in this sector

	All Respondents		Large Banks		Other Banks	
	Banks	Percent	Banks	Percent	Banks	Percent
Not important	15	29.4	9	27.3	6	33.3
Somewhat important	28	54.9	20	60.6	8	44.4
Very important	8	15.7	4	12.1	4	22.2
Total	51	100.0	33	100.0	18	100.0

f. Tightening underwriting policies on new loans or credit lines made to firms in other sectors

	All Respondents		Large Banks		Other Banks	
	Banks	Percent	Banks	Percent	Banks	Percent
Not important	36	70.6	26	78.8	10	55.6
Somewhat important	10	19.6	6	18.2	4	22.2
Very important	5	9.8	1	3.0	4	22.2
Total	51	100.0	33	100.0	18	100.0

Questions 10-15 ask about changes in standards and demand over the ***past three months*** for three different types of CRE loans at your bank: construction and land development loans, loans secured by nonfarm nonresidential properties, and loans secured by multifamily residential properties. Please report changes in enforcement of existing policies as changes in policies.

10. Over the past three months, how have your bank's credit standards for approving new applications for construction and land development loans or credit lines changed?

	All Respondents		Large Banks		Other Banks	
	Banks	Percent	Banks	Percent	Banks	Percent
Tightened considerably	0	0.0	0	0.0	0	0.0
Tightened somewhat	3	4.0	1	2.5	2	5.7
Remained basically unchanged	67	89.3	36	90.0	31	88.6
Eased somewhat	5	6.7	3	7.5	2	5.7
Eased considerably	0	0.0	0	0.0	0	0.0
Total	75	100.0	40	100.0	35	100.0

11. Over the past three months, how have your bank's credit standards for approving new applications for loans secured by nonfarm nonresidential properties changed?

	All Respondents		Large Banks		Other Banks	
	Banks	Percent	Banks	Percent	Banks	Percent
Tightened considerably	0	0.0	0	0.0	0	0.0
Tightened somewhat	2	2.6	0	0.0	2	5.7
Remained basically unchanged	66	86.8	35	85.4	31	88.6
Eased somewhat	8	10.5	6	14.6	2	5.7
Eased considerably	0	0.0	0	0.0	0	0.0
Total	76	100.0	41	100.0	35	100.0

12. Over the past three months, how have your bank's credit standards for approving new applications for loans secured by multifamily residential properties changed?

	All Respondents		Large Banks		Other Banks	
	Banks	Percent	Banks	Percent	Banks	Percent
Tightened considerably	0	0.0	0	0.0	0	0.0
Tightened somewhat	12	16.0	6	15.0	6	17.1
Remained basically unchanged	54	72.0	27	67.5	27	77.1
Eased somewhat	9	12.0	7	17.5	2	5.7
Eased considerably	0	0.0	0	0.0	0	0.0
Total	75	100.0	40	100.0	35	100.0

13. Apart from normal seasonal variation, how has demand for construction and land development loans changed over the past three months? (Please consider the number of requests for new spot loans, for disbursement of funds under existing loan commitments, and for new or increased credit lines.)

	All Respondents		Large Banks		Other Banks	
	Banks	Percent	Banks	Percent	Banks	Percent
Substantially stronger	0	0.0	0	0.0	0	0.0
Moderately stronger	19	25.3	8	20.0	11	31.4
About the same	52	69.3	30	75.0	22	62.9
Moderately weaker	4	5.3	2	5.0	2	5.7
Substantially weaker	0	0.0	0	0.0	0	0.0
Total	75	100.0	40	100.0	35	100.0

14. Apart from normal seasonal variation, how has demand for loans secured by nonfarm nonresidential properties changed over the past three months? (Please consider the number of requests for new spot loans, for disbursement of funds under existing loan commitments, and for new or increased credit lines.)

	All Respondents		Large Banks		Other Banks	
	Banks	Percent	Banks	Percent	Banks	Percent
Substantially stronger	1	1.3	1	2.4	0	0.0
Moderately stronger	10	13.2	7	17.1	3	8.6
About the same	63	82.9	32	78.0	31	88.6
Moderately weaker	2	2.6	1	2.4	1	2.9
Substantially weaker	0	0.0	0	0.0	0	0.0
Total	76	100.0	41	100.0	35	100.0

15. Apart from normal seasonal variation, how has demand for loans secured by multifamily residential properties changed over the past three months? (Please consider the number of requests for new spot loans, for disbursement of funds under existing loan commitments, and for new or increased credit lines.)

	All Respondents		Large Banks		Other Banks	
	Banks	Percent	Banks	Percent	Banks	Percent
Substantially stronger	2	2.7	1	2.5	1	2.9
Moderately stronger	18	24.0	9	22.5	9	25.7
About the same	46	61.3	23	57.5	23	65.7
Moderately weaker	9	12.0	7	17.5	2	5.7
Substantially weaker	0	0.0	0	0.0	0	0.0
Total	75	100.0	40	100.0	35	100.0

16. Over the past year, how has your bank changed the following policies on CRE loans? (Please assign *each* policy a number between 1 and 5 using the following scale: 1=tightened considerably, 2=tightened somewhat, 3=remained basically unchanged, 4=eased somewhat, 5=eased considerably.)

a. Maximum loan size

	All Respondents		Large Banks		Other Banks	
	Banks	Percent	Banks	Percent	Banks	Percent
Tightened considerably	1	1.3	0	0.0	1	2.9
Tightened somewhat	2	2.6	0	0.0	2	5.7
Remained basically unchanged	55	72.4	25	61.0	30	85.7
Eased somewhat	18	23.7	16	39.0	2	5.7
Eased considerably	0	0.0	0	0.0	0	0.0
Total	76	100.0	41	100.0	35	100.0

b. Maximum loan maturity

	All Respondents		Large Banks		Other Banks	
	Banks	Percent	Banks	Percent	Banks	Percent
Tightened considerably	1	1.3	0	0.0	1	2.9
Tightened somewhat	2	2.6	0	0.0	2	5.7
Remained basically unchanged	57	75.0	28	68.3	29	82.9
Eased somewhat	16	21.1	13	31.7	3	8.6
Eased considerably	0	0.0	0	0.0	0	0.0
Total	76	100.0	41	100.0	35	100.0

c. Spreads of loan rates over your bank's cost of funds (wider spreads=tightened; narrower spreads=eased)

	All Respondents		Large Banks		Other Banks	
	Banks	Percent	Banks	Percent	Banks	Percent
Tightened considerably	1	1.3	0	0.0	1	2.9
Tightened somewhat	5	6.6	2	4.9	3	8.6
Remained basically unchanged	36	47.4	12	29.3	24	68.6
Eased somewhat	32	42.1	25	61.0	7	20.0
Eased considerably	2	2.6	2	4.9	0	0.0
Total	76	100.0	41	100.0	35	100.0

d. Loan-to-value ratios

	All Respondents		Large Banks		Other Banks	
	Banks	Percent	Banks	Percent	Banks	Percent
Tightened considerably	1	1.3	0	0.0	1	2.9
Tightened somewhat	2	2.6	0	0.0	2	5.7
Remained basically unchanged	69	90.8	38	92.7	31	88.6
Eased somewhat	4	5.3	3	7.3	1	2.9
Eased considerably	0	0.0	0	0.0	0	0.0
Total	76	100.0	41	100.0	35	100.0

e. Debt-service coverage ratios

	All Respondents		Large Banks		Other Banks	
	Banks	Percent	Banks	Percent	Banks	Percent
Tightened considerably	0	0.0	0	0.0	0	0.0
Tightened somewhat	4	5.3	0	0.0	4	11.4
Remained basically unchanged	68	89.5	37	90.2	31	88.6
Eased somewhat	3	3.9	3	7.3	0	0.0
Eased considerably	1	1.3	1	2.4	0	0.0
Total	76	100.0	41	100.0	35	100.0

f. Market areas served (reduced market areas=tightened; expanded market areas=eased)

	All Respondents		Large Banks		Other Banks	
	Banks	Percent	Banks	Percent	Banks	Percent
Tightened considerably	1	1.3	0	0.0	1	2.9
Tightened somewhat	1	1.3	1	2.4	0	0.0
Remained basically unchanged	63	82.9	34	82.9	29	82.9
Eased somewhat	11	14.5	6	14.6	5	14.3
Eased considerably	0	0.0	0	0.0	0	0.0
Total	76	100.0	41	100.0	35	100.0

17. If your bank has tightened or eased its credit policies on CRE loans over the past year (as described in question 16), please select the 4 most important reasons among all the possible reasons listed below and rank them in order of importance. (Please respond to either 17A, 17B, or both as appropriate and rank the 4 most important reasons using a scale ranging from 4=the most important to 1=the least important.)

A. Possible reasons for tightening credit policies on CRE loans over the past year:

	All Respondents	Large Banks	Other Banks
	Mean	Mean	Mean
Less favorable or more uncertain outlook for CRE property prices	2.1	1.0	2.3
Less favorable or more uncertain outlook for vacancy rates or other fundamentals on CRE properties	3.2	3.0	3.2
Less favorable or more uncertain capitalization rates (the ratio of current net operating income to the original sale price or current market value) on CRE properties	2.1	2.0	2.1
Less aggressive competition from other banks or non-bank lenders (other financial intermediaries or the capital markets)	4.0	4.0	-
Reduced tolerance for risk	3.0	-	3.0
Decreased ability to securitize CRE loans	2.5	-	2.5
Increased concerns about capital adequacy, liquidity position, or regulation more broadly	2.2	3.0	2.0
Other	3.5	4.0	3.0
Number of respondents	12	3	9

B. Possible reasons for easing credit policies on CRE loans over the past year:

	All Respondents	Large Banks	Other Banks
	Mean	Mean	Mean
More favorable or less uncertain outlook for CRE property prices	2.5	2.4	2.6
More favorable or less uncertain outlook for vacancy rates or other fundamentals on CRE properties	2.5	2.5	2.7
More favorable or less uncertain capitalization rates (the ratio of current net operating income to the original sale price or current market value) on CRE properties	1.7	1.6	2.0
More aggressive competition from other banks or non-bank lenders (other financial intermediaries or the capital markets)	3.2	3.4	2.6
Increased tolerance for risk	2.5	2.8	1.8
Increased ability to securitize CRE loans	1.7	1.0	3.0
Decreased concerns about capital adequacy, liquidity position, or regulation more broadly	2.3	2.2	3.0
Other	3.0	2.0	4.0
Number of respondents	40	30	10

18. For each of the following categories of CRE lending, and assuming economic activity progresses in line with consensus forecasts, please indicate how you expect your bank's pace of loan originations during 2015 will change relative to its pace in 2014. (Please assign to *each* category a number between 1 and 6 using the following scale: 1=I expect the pace of originations at my bank will decline substantially; 2=I expect the pace of originations at my bank will decline somewhat; 3=I expect the pace of originations at my bank will be about the same; 4=I expect the pace of originations at my bank will increase somewhat; 5=I expect the pace of originations at my bank will increase substantially; 6=My bank does not originate this type of loan.)

a. Loans secured by nonfarm nonresidential properties

	All Respondents		Large Banks		Other Banks	
	Banks	Percent	Banks	Percent	Banks	Percent
I expect the pace of originations at my bank will decline substantially	2	2.6	2	4.9	0	0.0
I expect the pace of originations at my bank will decline somewhat	7	9.2	2	4.9	5	14.3
I expect the pace of originations at my bank will be about the same	46	60.5	24	58.5	22	62.9
I expect the pace of originations at my bank will increase somewhat	20	26.3	12	29.3	8	22.9
I expect the pace of originations at my bank will increase substantially	0	0.0	0	0.0	0	0.0
My bank does not originate this type of loan	1	1.3	1	2.4	0	0.0
Total	76	100.0	41	100.0	35	100.0

b. Loans secured by multifamily (5 or more) residential properties

	All Respondents		Large Banks		Other Banks	
	Banks	Percent	Banks	Percent	Banks	Percent
I expect the pace of originations at my bank will decline substantially	1	1.3	1	2.5	0	0.0
I expect the pace of originations at my bank will decline somewhat	22	29.3	14	35.0	8	22.9
I expect the pace of originations at my bank will be about the same	34	45.3	17	42.5	17	48.6
I expect the pace of originations at my bank will increase somewhat	15	20.0	6	15.0	9	25.7
I expect the pace of originations at my bank will increase substantially	2	2.7	1	2.5	1	2.9
My bank does not originate this type of loan	1	1.3	1	2.5	0	0.0
Total	75	100.0	40	100.0	35	100.0

c. 1-4 family residential construction loans

	All Respondents		Large Banks		Other Banks	
	Banks	Percent	Banks	Percent	Banks	Percent
I expect the pace of originations at my bank will decline substantially	0	0.0	0	0.0	0	0.0
I expect the pace of originations at my bank will decline somewhat	2	2.7	1	2.6	1	2.9
I expect the pace of originations at my bank will be about the same	45	61.6	27	69.2	18	52.9
I expect the pace of originations at my bank will increase somewhat	19	26.0	4	10.3	15	44.1
I expect the pace of originations at my bank will increase substantially	0	0.0	0	0.0	0	0.0
My bank does not originate this type of loan	7	9.6	7	17.9	0	0.0
Total	73	100.0	39	100.0	34	100.0

d. Other construction loans and all land development and other land loans

	All Respondents		Large Banks		Other Banks	
	Banks	Percent	Banks	Percent	Banks	Percent
I expect the pace of originations at my bank will decline substantially	1	1.4	1	2.6	0	0.0
I expect the pace of originations at my bank will decline somewhat	9	12.2	5	12.8	4	11.4
I expect the pace of originations at my bank will be about the same	53	71.6	29	74.4	24	68.6
I expect the pace of originations at my bank will increase somewhat	9	12.2	2	5.1	7	20.0
I expect the pace of originations at my bank will increase substantially	0	0.0	0	0.0	0	0.0
My bank does not originate this type of loan	2	2.7	2	5.1	0	0.0
Total	74	100.0	39	100.0	35	100.0

Note: *Beginning with the January 2015 survey, the loan categories referred to in the questions regarding changes in credit standards and demand for residential mortgage loans have been revised to reflect the Consumer Financial Protection Bureau's qualified mortgage rules.*

Questions 19-20 *ask about seven categories of* **residential mortgage loans** *at your bank: Government-Sponsored Enterprise eligible (GSE-eligible) residential mortgages, government residential mortgages, Qualified Mortgage non-jumbo non-GSE-eligible (QM non-jumbo, non-GSE-eligible) residential mortgages, QM jumbo residential mortgages, non-QM jumbo residential mortgages, non-QM non-jumbo residential mortgages, and subprime residential mortgages.*

For the purposes of this survey, please use the following definitions of these loan categories and include first-lien closed-end loans to purchase homes only. The loan categories have been defined so that every first-lien closed-end residential mortgage loan used for home purchase fits into one of the following seven categories:

- *The* **GSE-eligible** *category of residential mortgages includes loans that meet the underwriting guidelines, including loan limit amounts, of the GSEs - Fannie Mae and Freddie Mac.*

- *The* **government** *category of residential mortgages includes loans that are insured by the Federal Housing Administration, guaranteed by the Department of Veterans Affairs, or originated under government programs, including the U.S. Department of Agriculture home loan programs.*

- *The* **QM non-jumbo, non-GSE-eligible** *category of residential mortgages includes loans that satisfy the standards for a qualified mortgage and have loan balances that are below the loan limit amounts set by the GSEs but otherwise do not meet the GSE underwriting guidelines.*

- *The* **QM jumbo** *category of residential mortgages includes loans that satisfy the standards for a qualified mortgage but have loan balances that are above the loan limit amount set by the GSEs.*

- *The* **non-QM jumbo** *category of residential mortgages includes loans that do not satisfy the standards for a qualified mortgage and have loan balances that are above the loan limit amount set by the GSEs.*

- *The* **non-QM non-jumbo** *category of residential mortgages includes loans that do not satisfy the standards for a qualified mortgage and have loan balances that are below the loan limit amount set by the GSEs.(Please exclude loans classified by your bank as subprime in this category.)*

- *The* **subprime** *category of residential mortgages includes loans classified by your bank as subprime. This category typically includes loans made to borrowers with weakened credit* *histories that include payment delinquencies, charge-offs, judgements, and/or bankruptcies; reduced repayment capacity as measured by credit scores or debt-to-income ratios; or incomplete credit histories.*

Question 19 *deals with changes in your bank's credit standards for loans in each of the seven loan categories over the past three months. If your bank's credit standards have not changed over the relevant period, please report them as unchanged even if the standards are either restrictive or accommodative relative to longer-term norms. If your bank's credit standards have tightened or eased over the relevant period, please so report them regardless of how they stand relative to longer-term norms. Also, please report changes in enforcement of existing standards as changes in standards.* **Question 20** *deals with changes in demand for loans in each of the seven loan categories over the past three months.*

19. Over the past three months, how have your bank's credit standards for approving applications from individuals for mortgage loans to purchase homes changed? (Please consider only new originations as opposed to the refinancing of existing mortgages.)

   A. Credit standards on mortgage loans that your bank categorizes as GSE-eligible residential mortgages have:

	All Respondents		Large Banks		Other Banks	
	Banks	Percent	Banks	Percent	Banks	Percent
Tightened considerably	0	0.0	0	0.0	0	0.0
Tightened somewhat	2	2.9	1	2.9	1	2.9
Remained basically unchanged	52	76.5	24	70.6	28	82.4
Eased somewhat	13	19.1	8	23.5	5	14.7
Eased considerably	1	1.5	1	2.9	0	0.0
Total	68	100.0	34	100.0	34	100.0

   For this question, 4 respondents answered "My bank does not originate GSE-eligible residential mortgages."

B. Credit standards on mortgage loans that your bank categorizes as government residential mortgages have:

	All Respondents		Large Banks		Other Banks	
	Banks	Percent	Banks	Percent	Banks	Percent
Tightened considerably	0	0.0	0	0.0	0	0.0
Tightened somewhat	1	1.6	1	3.1	0	0.0
Remained basically unchanged	53	84.1	27	84.4	26	83.9
Eased somewhat	8	12.7	3	9.4	5	16.1
Eased considerably	1	1.6	1	3.1	0	0.0
Total	63	100.0	32	100.0	31	100.0

For this question, 9 respondents answered "My bank does not originate government residential mortgages."

C. Credit standards on mortgage loans that your bank categorizes as QM non-jumbo, non-GSE-eligible residential mortgages have:

	All Respondents		Large Banks		Other Banks	
	Banks	Percent	Banks	Percent	Banks	Percent
Tightened considerably	0	0.0	0	0.0	0	0.0
Tightened somewhat	2	3.4	1	3.4	1	3.4
Remained basically unchanged	54	93.1	28	96.6	26	89.7
Eased somewhat	2	3.4	0	0.0	2	6.9
Eased considerably	0	0.0	0	0.0	0	0.0
Total	58	100.0	29	100.0	29	100.0

For this question, 14 respondents answered "My bank does not originate QM non-jumbo, non-GSE-eligible residential mortgages."

D. Credit standards on mortgage loans that your bank categorizes as QM jumbo residential mortgages have:

	All Respondents		Large Banks		Other Banks	
	Banks	Percent	Banks	Percent	Banks	Percent
Tightened considerably	0	0.0	0	0.0	0	0.0
Tightened somewhat	1	1.5	1	2.9	0	0.0
Remained basically unchanged	58	86.6	28	82.4	30	90.9
Eased somewhat	8	11.9	5	14.7	3	9.1
Eased considerably	0	0.0	0	0.0	0	0.0
Total	67	100.0	34	100.0	33	100.0

For this question, 5 respondents answered "My bank does not originate QM jumbo residential mortgages."

E. Credit standards on mortgage loans that your bank categorizes as non-QM jumbo residential mortgages have:

	All Respondents		Large Banks		Other Banks	
	Banks	Percent	Banks	Percent	Banks	Percent
Tightened considerably	0	0.0	0	0.0	0	0.0
Tightened somewhat	1	1.6	0	0.0	1	3.6
Remained basically unchanged	58	92.1	31	88.6	27	96.4
Eased somewhat	4	6.3	4	11.4	0	0.0
Eased considerably	0	0.0	0	0.0	0	0.0
Total	63	100.0	35	100.0	28	100.0

For this question, 9 respondents answered "My bank does not originate non-QM jumbo residential mortgages."

F. Credit standards on mortgage loans that your bank categorizes as non-QM non-jumbo residential mortgages have:

	All Respondents		Large Banks		Other Banks	
	Banks	Percent	Banks	Percent	Banks	Percent
Tightened considerably	0	0.0	0	0.0	0	0.0
Tightened somewhat	0	0.0	0	0.0	0	0.0
Remained basically unchanged	58	98.3	31	96.9	27	100.0
Eased somewhat	1	1.7	1	3.1	0	0.0
Eased considerably	0	0.0	0	0.0	0	0.0
Total	59	100.0	32	100.0	27	100.0

For this question, 13 respondents answered "My bank does not originate non-QM non-jumbo residential mortgages."

G. Credit standards on mortgage loans that your bank categorizes as subprime residential mortgages have:

	All Respondents		Large Banks		Other Banks	
	Banks	Percent	Banks	Percent	Banks	Percent
Tightened considerably	0	0.0	0	0.0	0	0.0
Tightened somewhat	1	16.7	0	0.0	1	20.0
Remained basically unchanged	5	83.3	1	100.0	4	80.0
Eased somewhat	0	0.0	0	0.0	0	0.0
Eased considerably	0	0.0	0	0.0	0	0.0
Total	6	100.0	1	100.0	5	100.0

For this question, 66 respondents answered "My bank does not originate subprime residential mortgages."

20. Apart from normal seasonal variation, how has demand for mortgages to purchase homes changed over the past three months? (Please consider only applications for new originations as opposed to applications for refinancing of existing mortgages.)

A. Demand for mortgages that your bank categorizes as GSE-eligible residential mortgages was:

	All Respondents		Large Banks		Other Banks	
	Banks	Percent	Banks	Percent	Banks	Percent
Substantially stronger	4	5.9	2	5.9	2	5.9
Moderately stronger	30	44.1	14	41.2	16	47.1
About the same	31	45.6	16	47.1	15	44.1
Moderately weaker	3	4.4	2	5.9	1	2.9
Substantially weaker	0	0.0	0	0.0	0	0.0
Total	68	100.0	34	100.0	34	100.0

For this question, 4 respondents answered "My bank does not originate GSE-eligible residential mortgages."

B. Demand for mortgages that your bank categorizes as government residential mortgages was:

	All Respondents		Large Banks		Other Banks	
	Banks	Percent	Banks	Percent	Banks	Percent
Substantially stronger	0	0.0	0	0.0	0	0.0
Moderately stronger	29	46.0	15	46.9	14	45.2
About the same	30	47.6	14	43.8	16	51.6
Moderately weaker	4	6.3	3	9.4	1	3.2
Substantially weaker	0	0.0	0	0.0	0	0.0
Total	63	100.0	32	100.0	31	100.0

For this question, 9 respondents answered "My bank does not originate government residential mortgages."

C. Demand for mortgages that your bank categorizes as QM non-jumbo, non-GSE-eligible residential mortgages was:

	All Respondents		Large Banks		Other Banks	
	Banks	Percent	Banks	Percent	Banks	Percent
Substantially stronger	0	0.0	0	0.0	0	0.0
Moderately stronger	18	31.0	9	31.0	9	31.0
About the same	36	62.1	18	62.1	18	62.1
Moderately weaker	3	5.2	2	6.9	1	3.4
Substantially weaker	1	1.7	0	0.0	1	3.4
Total	58	100.0	29	100.0	29	100.0

For this question, 14 respondents answered "My bank does not originate QM non-jumbo, non-GSE-eligible residential mortgages."

D. Demand for mortgages that your bank categorizes as QM jumbo residential mortgages was:

	All Respondents		Large Banks		Other Banks	
	Banks	Percent	Banks	Percent	Banks	Percent
Substantially stronger	3	4.5	2	5.9	1	3.0
Moderately stronger	15	22.4	9	26.5	6	18.2
About the same	45	67.2	20	58.8	25	75.8
Moderately weaker	4	6.0	3	8.8	1	3.0
Substantially weaker	0	0.0	0	0.0	0	0.0
Total	67	100.0	34	100.0	33	100.0

For this question, 5 respondents answered "My bank does not originate QM jumbo residential mortgages."

E. Demand for mortgages that your bank categorizes as non-QM jumbo residential mortgages was:

	All Respondents		Large Banks		Other Banks	
	Banks	Percent	Banks	Percent	Banks	Percent
Substantially stronger	2	3.2	2	5.7	0	0.0
Moderately stronger	9	14.3	6	17.1	3	10.7
About the same	47	74.6	24	68.6	23	82.1
Moderately weaker	3	4.8	3	8.6	0	0.0
Substantially weaker	2	3.2	0	0.0	2	7.1
Total	63	100.0	35	100.0	28	100.0

For this question, 9 respondents answered "My bank does not originate non-QM jumbo residential mortgages."

F. Demand for mortgages that your bank categorizes as non-QM non-jumbo residential mortgages was:

	All Respondents		Large Banks		Other Banks	
	Banks	Percent	Banks	Percent	Banks	Percent
Substantially stronger	0	0.0	0	0.0	0	0.0
Moderately stronger	8	13.6	6	18.8	2	7.4
About the same	48	81.4	24	75.0	24	88.9
Moderately weaker	2	3.4	2	6.3	0	0.0
Substantially weaker	1	1.7	0	0.0	1	3.7
Total	59	100.0	32	100.0	27	100.0

For this question, 13 respondents answered "My bank does not originate non-QM non-jumbo residential mortgages."

G. Demand for mortgages that your bank categorizes as subprime residential mortgages was:

	All Respondents		Large Banks		Other Banks	
	Banks	Percent	Banks	Percent	Banks	Percent
Substantially stronger	0	0.0	0	0.0	0	0.0
Moderately stronger	0	0.0	0	0.0	0	0.0
About the same	6	100.0	1	100.0	5	100.0
Moderately weaker	0	0.0	0	0.0	0	0.0
Substantially weaker	0	0.0	0	0.0	0	0.0
Total	6	100.0	1	100.0	5	100.0

For this question, 66 respondents answered "My bank does not originate subprime residential mortgages."

Questions 21-22 ask about **revolving home equity lines of credit** at your bank. *Question 21 deals with changes in your bank's credit standards over the past three months. Question 22 deals with changes in demand. If your bank's credit standards have not changed over the relevant period, please report them as unchanged even if they are either restrictive or accommodative relative to longer-term norms. If your bank's credit standards have tightened or eased over the relevant period, please so report them regardless of how they stand relative to longer-term norms. Also, please report changes in enforcement of existing standards as changes in standards.*

21. Over the past three months, how have your bank's credit standards for approving applications for revolving home equity lines of credit changed?

	All Respondents		Large Banks		Other Banks	
	Banks	Percent	Banks	Percent	Banks	Percent
Tightened considerably	1	1.4	0	0.0	1	2.9
Tightened somewhat	1	1.4	1	2.6	0	0.0
Remained basically unchanged	60	83.3	33	86.8	27	79.4
Eased somewhat	10	13.9	4	10.5	6	17.6
Eased considerably	0	0.0	0	0.0	0	0.0
Total	72	100.0	38	100.0	34	100.0

22. Apart from normal seasonal variation, how has demand for revolving home equity lines of credit changed over the past three months? (Please consider only funds actually disbursed as opposed to requests for new or increased lines of credit.)

	All Respondents		Large Banks		Other Banks	
	Banks	Percent	Banks	Percent	Banks	Percent
Substantially stronger	1	1.4	0	0.0	1	2.9
Moderately stronger	16	22.2	7	18.4	9	26.5
About the same	47	65.3	27	71.1	20	58.8
Moderately weaker	8	11.1	4	10.5	4	11.8
Substantially weaker	0	0.0	0	0.0	0	0.0
Total	72	100.0	38	100.0	34	100.0

On November 20, 2014, Fannie Mae and Freddie Mac, at the direction of the Federal Housing Finance Agency, issued guidelines on the definition of life-of-loan representation and warranty exclusions. The following question asks about changes in your bank's lending policies in response to these guidelines.

23. How much more or less likely is your bank to approve an application for a 30-year fixed-rate GSE-eligible home purchase mortgage loan to a borrower with the stated FICO score (or equivalent) and down payment in the current environment than it would have been if the guidelines had not been issued? In each case, assume that all other characteristics of the borrower and the property are typical for loan applications that are eligible for sale to the GSEs with that FICO score (or equivalent) and down payment. (Please assign *each* borrower category a number between 1 and 5 using the following scale: 1=much less likely, 2=somewhat less likely, 3=about the same, 4=somewhat more likely, 5=much more likely.)

a. A borrower with a FICO score (or equivalent) of 620 and a down payment of 20 percent

	All Respondents		Large Banks		Other Banks	
	Banks	Percent	Banks	Percent	Banks	Percent
Much less likely	4	6.3	1	3.0	3	10.0
Somehwat less likely	3	4.8	0	0.0	3	10.0
About the same	52	82.5	29	87.9	23	76.7
Somewhat more likely	4	6.3	3	9.1	1	3.3
Much more likely	0	0.0	0	0.0	0	0.0
Total	63	100.0	33	100.0	30	100.0

b. A borrower with a FICO score (or equivalent) of 680 and a down payment of 20 percent

	All Respondents		Large Banks		Other Banks	
	Banks	Percent	Banks	Percent	Banks	Percent
Much less likely	0	0.0	0	0.0	0	0.0
Somehwat less likely	2	3.2	1	3.0	1	3.3
About the same	56	88.9	30	90.9	26	86.7
Somewhat more likely	4	6.3	2	6.1	2	6.7
Much more likely	1	1.6	0	0.0	1	3.3
Total	63	100.0	33	100.0	30	100.0

c. A borrower with a FICO score (or equivalent) of 620 and a down payment of 10 percent

	All Respondents		Large Banks		Other Banks	
	Banks	Percent	Banks	Percent	Banks	Percent
Much less likely	6	9.5	1	3.0	5	16.7
Somehwat less likely	7	11.1	1	3.0	6	20.0
About the same	46	73.0	28	84.8	18	60.0
Somewhat more likely	4	6.3	3	9.1	1	3.3
Much more likely	0	0.0	0	0.0	0	0.0
Total	63	100.0	33	100.0	30	100.0

d. A borrower with a FICO score (or equivalent) of 680 and a down payment of 10 percent

	All Respondents		Large Banks		Other Banks	
	Banks	Percent	Banks	Percent	Banks	Percent
Much less likely	1	1.6	1	3.0	0	0.0
Somehwat less likely	1	1.6	0	0.0	1	3.3
About the same	56	88.9	28	84.8	28	93.3
Somewhat more likely	4	6.3	4	12.1	0	0.0
Much more likely	1	1.6	0	0.0	1	3.3
Total	63	100.0	33	100.0	30	100.0

e. A borrower with a FICO score (or equivalent) of 720 and a down payment of 10 percent

	All Respondents		Large Banks		Other Banks	
	Banks	Percent	Banks	Percent	Banks	Percent
Much less likely	0	0.0	0	0.0	0	0.0
Somehwat less likely	1	1.6	0	0.0	1	3.2
About the same	56	87.5	30	90.9	26	83.9
Somewhat more likely	6	9.4	3	9.1	3	9.7
Much more likely	1	1.6	0	0.0	1	3.2
Total	64	100.0	33	100.0	31	100.0

f. A borrower with a FICO score (or equivalent) of 620 and a down payment of 5 percent

	All Respondents		Large Banks		Other Banks	
	Banks	Percent	Banks	Percent	Banks	Percent
Much less likely	9	14.3	2	6.1	7	23.3
Somehwat less likely	3	4.8	0	0.0	3	10.0
About the same	47	74.6	28	84.8	19	63.3
Somewhat more likely	4	6.3	3	9.1	1	3.3
Much more likely	0	0.0	0	0.0	0	0.0
Total	63	100.0	33	100.0	30	100.0

g. A borrower with a FICO score (or equivalent) of 680 and a down payment of 5 percent

	All Respondents		Large Banks		Other Banks	
	Banks	Percent	Banks	Percent	Banks	Percent
Much less likely	1	1.6	1	3.0	0	0.0
Somehwat less likely	5	7.9	1	3.0	4	13.3
About the same	50	79.4	28	84.8	22	73.3
Somewhat more likely	7	11.1	3	9.1	4	13.3
Much more likely	0	0.0	0	0.0	0	0.0
Total	63	100.0	33	100.0	30	100.0

Questions 24-33 ask about consumer lending at your bank. Question 24 deals with changes in your bank's willingness to make consumer loans over the past three months. Questions 25-30 deal with changes in credit standards and loan terms over the same period. Questions 31-33 deal with changes in demand for consumer loans over the past three months. If your bank's lending policies have not changed over the past three months, please report them as unchanged even if the policies are either restrictive or accommodative relative to longer-term norms. If your bank's policies have tightened or eased over the past three months, please so report them regardless of how they stand relative to longer-term norms. Also, please report changes in enforcement of existing policies as changes in policies.

24. Please indicate your bank's willingness to make consumer installment loans now as opposed to three months ago.

	All Respondents		Large Banks		Other Banks	
	Banks	Percent	Banks	Percent	Banks	Percent
Much more willing	0	0.0	0	0.0	0	0.0
Somewhat more willing	7	9.7	4	10.8	3	8.6
About unchanged	64	88.9	33	89.2	31	88.6
Somewhat less willing	1	1.4	0	0.0	1	2.9
Much less willing	0	0.0	0	0.0	0	0.0
Total	72	100.0	37	100.0	35	100.0

25. Over the past three months, how have your bank's credit standards for approving applications for credit cards from individuals or households changed?

	All Respondents		Large Banks		Other Banks	
	Banks	Percent	Banks	Percent	Banks	Percent
Tightened considerably	0	0.0	0	0.0	0	0.0
Tightened somewhat	0	0.0	0	0.0	0	0.0
Remained basically unchanged	54	98.2	32	97.0	22	100.0
Eased somewhat	1	1.8	1	3.0	0	0.0
Eased considerably	0	0.0	0	0.0	0	0.0
Total	55	100.0	33	100.0	22	100.0

26. Over the past three months, how have your bank's credit standards for approving applications for auto loans to individuals or households changed? (Please include loans arising from retail sales of passenger cars and other vehicles such as minivans, vans, sport-utility vehicles, pickup trucks, and similar light trucks for personal use, whether new or used. Please exclude loans to finance fleet sales, personal cash loans secured by automobiles already paid for, loans to finance the purchase of commercial vehicles and farm equipment, and lease financing.)

	All Respondents		Large Banks		Other Banks	
	Banks	Percent	Banks	Percent	Banks	Percent
Tightened considerably	0	0.0	0	0.0	0	0.0
Tightened somewhat	1	1.5	0	0.0	1	2.9
Remained basically unchanged	60	90.9	28	87.5	32	94.1
Eased somewhat	5	7.6	4	12.5	1	2.9
Eased considerably	0	0.0	0	0.0	0	0.0
Total	66	100.0	32	100.0	34	100.0

27. Over the past three months, how have your bank's credit standards for approving applications for consumer loans other than credit card and auto loans changed?

	All Respondents		Large Banks		Other Banks	
	Banks	Percent	Banks	Percent	Banks	Percent
Tightened considerably	0	0.0	0	0.0	0	0.0
Tightened somewhat	1	1.4	1	2.7	0	0.0
Remained basically unchanged	66	91.7	32	86.5	34	97.1
Eased somewhat	5	6.9	4	10.8	1	2.9
Eased considerably	0	0.0	0	0.0	0	0.0
Total	72	100.0	37	100.0	35	100.0

28. Over the past three months, how has your bank changed the following terms and conditions on new or existing credit card accounts for individuals or households?

    a. Credit limits

	All Respondents		Large Banks		Other Banks	
	Banks	Percent	Banks	Percent	Banks	Percent
Tightened considerably	0	0.0	0	0.0	0	0.0
Tightened somewhat	0	0.0	0	0.0	0	0.0
Remained basically unchanged	49	94.2	28	90.3	21	100.0
Eased somewhat	3	5.8	3	9.7	0	0.0
Eased considerably	0	0.0	0	0.0	0	0.0
Total	52	100.0	31	100.0	21	100.0

    b. Spreads of interest rates charged on outstanding balances over your bank's cost of funds (wider spreads=tightened, narrower spreads=eased)

	All Respondents		Large Banks		Other Banks	
	Banks	Percent	Banks	Percent	Banks	Percent
Tightened considerably	0	0.0	0	0.0	0	0.0
Tightened somewhat	2	3.8	2	6.5	0	0.0
Remained basically unchanged	50	96.2	29	93.5	21	100.0
Eased somewhat	0	0.0	0	0.0	0	0.0
Eased considerably	0	0.0	0	0.0	0	0.0
Total	52	100.0	31	100.0	21	100.0

c. Minimum percent of outstanding balances required to be repaid each month

	All Respondents		Large Banks		Other Banks	
	Banks	Percent	Banks	Percent	Banks	Percent
Tightened considerably	0	0.0	0	0.0	0	0.0
Tightened somewhat	0	0.0	0	0.0	0	0.0
Remained basically unchanged	52	100.0	31	100.0	21	100.0
Eased somewhat	0	0.0	0	0.0	0	0.0
Eased considerably	0	0.0	0	0.0	0	0.0
Total	52	100.0	31	100.0	21	100.0

d. Minimum required credit score (increased score=tightened, reduced score=eased)

	All Respondents		Large Banks		Other Banks	
	Banks	Percent	Banks	Percent	Banks	Percent
Tightened considerably	0	0.0	0	0.0	0	0.0
Tightened somewhat	0	0.0	0	0.0	0	0.0
Remained basically unchanged	50	96.2	29	93.5	21	100.0
Eased somewhat	2	3.8	2	6.5	0	0.0
Eased considerably	0	0.0	0	0.0	0	0.0
Total	52	100.0	31	100.0	21	100.0

e. The extent to which loans are granted to some customers that do not meet credit scoring thresholds (increased=eased, decreased=tightened)

	All Respondents		Large Banks		Other Banks	
	Banks	Percent	Banks	Percent	Banks	Percent
Tightened considerably	0	0.0	0	0.0	0	0.0
Tightened somewhat	3	5.9	2	6.7	1	4.8
Remained basically unchanged	46	90.2	27	90.0	19	90.5
Eased somewhat	2	3.9	1	3.3	1	4.8
Eased considerably	0	0.0	0	0.0	0	0.0
Total	51	100.0	30	100.0	21	100.0

29. Over the past three months, how has your bank changed the following terms and conditions on loans to individuals or households to purchase autos?

   a. Maximum maturity

	All Respondents		Large Banks		Other Banks	
	Banks	Percent	Banks	Percent	Banks	Percent
Tightened considerably	0	0.0	0	0.0	0	0.0
Tightened somewhat	0	0.0	0	0.0	0	0.0
Remained basically unchanged	62	92.5	31	93.9	31	91.2
Eased somewhat	5	7.5	2	6.1	3	8.8
Eased considerably	0	0.0	0	0.0	0	0.0
Total	67	100.0	33	100.0	34	100.0

b. Spreads of loan rates over your bank's cost of funds (wider spreads=tightened, narrower spreads=eased)

	All Respondents		Large Banks		Other Banks	
	Banks	Percent	Banks	Percent	Banks	Percent
Tightened considerably	0	0.0	0	0.0	0	0.0
Tightened somewhat	4	6.0	4	12.1	0	0.0
Remained basically unchanged	51	76.1	23	69.7	28	82.4
Eased somewhat	11	16.4	5	15.2	6	17.6
Eased considerably	1	1.5	1	3.0	0	0.0
Total	67	100.0	33	100.0	34	100.0

c. Minimum required down payment (higher=tightened, lower=eased)

	All Respondents		Large Banks		Other Banks	
	Banks	Percent	Banks	Percent	Banks	Percent
Tightened considerably	0	0.0	0	0.0	0	0.0
Tightened somewhat	1	1.5	0	0.0	1	2.9
Remained basically unchanged	65	97.0	32	97.0	33	97.1
Eased somewhat	1	1.5	1	3.0	0	0.0
Eased considerably	0	0.0	0	0.0	0	0.0
Total	67	100.0	33	100.0	34	100.0

d. Minimum required credit score (increased score=tightened, reduced score=eased)

	All Respondents		Large Banks		Other Banks	
	Banks	Percent	Banks	Percent	Banks	Percent
Tightened considerably	0	0.0	0	0.0	0	0.0
Tightened somewhat	0	0.0	0	0.0	0	0.0
Remained basically unchanged	64	95.5	30	90.9	34	100.0
Eased somewhat	3	4.5	3	9.1	0	0.0
Eased considerably	0	0.0	0	0.0	0	0.0
Total	67	100.0	33	100.0	34	100.0

e. The extent to which loans are granted to some customers that do not meet credit scoring thresholds (increased=eased, decreased=tightened)

	All Respondents		Large Banks		Other Banks	
	Banks	Percent	Banks	Percent	Banks	Percent
Tightened considerably	0	0.0	0	0.0	0	0.0
Tightened somewhat	1	1.5	0	0.0	1	2.9
Remained basically unchanged	65	97.0	32	97.0	33	97.1
Eased somewhat	1	1.5	1	3.0	0	0.0
Eased considerably	0	0.0	0	0.0	0	0.0
Total	67	100.0	33	100.0	34	100.0

30. Over the past three months, how has your bank changed the following terms and conditions on consumer loans *other than* credit card and auto loans?

a. Maximum maturity

	All Respondents		Large Banks		Other Banks	
	Banks	Percent	Banks	Percent	Banks	Percent
Tightened considerably	0	0.0	0	0.0	0	0.0
Tightened somewhat	1	1.4	0	0.0	1	2.9
Remained basically unchanged	71	98.6	37	100.0	34	97.1
Eased somewhat	0	0.0	0	0.0	0	0.0
Eased considerably	0	0.0	0	0.0	0	0.0
Total	72	100.0	37	100.0	35	100.0

b. Spreads of loan rates over your bank's cost of funds (wider spreads=tightened, narrower spreads=eased)

	All Respondents		Large Banks		Other Banks	
	Banks	Percent	Banks	Percent	Banks	Percent
Tightened considerably	0	0.0	0	0.0	0	0.0
Tightened somewhat	2	2.8	2	5.4	0	0.0
Remained basically unchanged	64	88.9	34	91.9	30	85.7
Eased somewhat	6	8.3	1	2.7	5	14.3
Eased considerably	0	0.0	0	0.0	0	0.0
Total	72	100.0	37	100.0	35	100.0

c. Minimum required down payment (higher=tightened, lower=eased)

	All Respondents		Large Banks		Other Banks	
	Banks	Percent	Banks	Percent	Banks	Percent
Tightened considerably	0	0.0	0	0.0	0	0.0
Tightened somewhat	0	0.0	0	0.0	0	0.0
Remained basically unchanged	72	100.0	37	100.0	35	100.0
Eased somewhat	0	0.0	0	0.0	0	0.0
Eased considerably	0	0.0	0	0.0	0	0.0
Total	72	100.0	37	100.0	35	100.0

d. Minimum required credit score (increased score=tightened, reduced score=eased)

	All Respondents		Large Banks		Other Banks	
	Banks	Percent	Banks	Percent	Banks	Percent
Tightened considerably	0	0.0	0	0.0	0	0.0
Tightened somewhat	0	0.0	0	0.0	0	0.0
Remained basically unchanged	71	98.6	36	97.3	35	100.0
Eased somewhat	1	1.4	1	2.7	0	0.0
Eased considerably	0	0.0	0	0.0	0	0.0
Total	72	100.0	37	100.0	35	100.0

e. The extent to which loans are granted to some customers that do not meet credit scoring thresholds (increased=eased, decreased=tightened)

	All Respondents		Large Banks		Other Banks	
	Banks	Percent	Banks	Percent	Banks	Percent
Tightened considerably	0	0.0	0	0.0	0	0.0
Tightened somewhat	2	2.8	0	0.0	2	5.7
Remained basically unchanged	70	97.2	37	100.0	33	94.3
Eased somewhat	0	0.0	0	0.0	0	0.0
Eased considerably	0	0.0	0	0.0	0	0.0
Total	72	100.0	37	100.0	35	100.0

31. Apart from normal seasonal variation, how has demand from individuals or households for credit card loans changed over the past three months?

	All Respondents		Large Banks		Other Banks	
	Banks	Percent	Banks	Percent	Banks	Percent
Substantially stronger	0	0.0	0	0.0	0	0.0
Moderately stronger	8	15.4	5	16.1	3	14.3
About the same	41	78.8	25	80.6	16	76.2
Moderately weaker	3	5.8	1	3.2	2	9.5
Substantially weaker	0	0.0	0	0.0	0	0.0
Total	52	100.0	31	100.0	21	100.0

32. Apart from normal seasonal variation, how has demand from individuals or households for auto loans changed over the past three months?

	All Respondents		Large Banks		Other Banks	
	Banks	Percent	Banks	Percent	Banks	Percent
Substantially stronger	1	1.5	1	3.0	0	0.0
Moderately stronger	13	19.4	5	15.2	8	23.5
About the same	45	67.2	22	66.7	23	67.6
Moderately weaker	8	11.9	5	15.2	3	8.8
Substantially weaker	0	0.0	0	0.0	0	0.0
Total	67	100.0	33	100.0	34	100.0

33. Apart from normal seasonal variation, how has demand from individuals or households for consumer loans other than credit card and auto loans changed over the past three months?

	All Respondents		Large Banks		Other Banks	
	Banks	Percent	Banks	Percent	Banks	Percent
Substantially stronger	0	0.0	0	0.0	0	0.0
Moderately stronger	2	2.8	1	2.7	1	2.9
About the same	67	93.1	35	94.6	32	91.4
Moderately weaker	3	4.2	1	2.7	2	5.7
Substantially weaker	0	0.0	0	0.0	0	0.0
Total	72	100.0	37	100.0	35	100.0

1. The sample is selected from among the largest banks in each Federal Reserve District. In the table, large banks are defined as those with total domestic assets of $20 billion or more as of December 31, 2014. The combined assets of the 41 large banks totaled $9.1 trillion, compared to $9.4 trillion for the entire panel of 76 banks, and $ 12.9 trillion for all domestically chartered, federally insured commercial banks.

Table 2

Senior Loan Officer Opinion Survey on Bank Lending Practices at Selected Branches and Agencies of Foreign Banks in the United States [1]

(Status of policy as of April 2015)

Questions 1-6 *ask about commercial and industrial (C&I) loans at your bank. Questions 1-3 deal with changes in your bank's lending policies over the past three months. Questions 4-5 deal with changes in demand for C&I loans over the past three months. Question 6 asks about changes in prospective demand for C&I loans at your bank, as indicated by the volume of recent inquiries about the availability of new credit lines or increases in existing lines. If your bank's lending policies have not changed over the past three months, please report them as unchanged even if the policies are either restrictive or accommodative relative to longer-term norms. If your bank's policies have tightened or eased over the past three months, please so report them regardless of how they stand relative to longer-term norms. Also, please report changes in enforcement of existing policies as changes in policies.*

1. Over the past three months, how have your bank's credit standards for approving applications for C&I loans or credit lines—other than those to be used to finance mergers and acquisitions—changed?

	All Respondents	
	Banks	Percent
Tightened considerably	0	0.0
Tightened somewhat	1	4.3
Remained basically unchanged	20	87.0
Eased somewhat	2	8.7
Eased considerably	0	0.0
Total	23	100.0

2. For applications for C&I loans or credit lines—other than those to be used to finance mergers and acquisitions—that your bank currently is willing to approve, how have the terms of those loans changed over the past three months?

   a. Maximum size of credit lines

	All Respondents	
	Banks	Percent
Tightened considerably	0	0.0
Tightened somewhat	0	0.0
Remained basically unchanged	20	87.0
Eased somewhat	3	13.0
Eased considerably	0	0.0
Total	23	100.0

   b. Maximum maturity of loans or credit lines

	All Respondents	
	Banks	Percent
Tightened considerably	0	0.0
Tightened somewhat	0	0.0
Remained basically unchanged	22	100.0
Eased somewhat	0	0.0
Eased considerably	0	0.0
Total	22	100.0

c. Costs of credit lines

	All Respondents	
	Banks	Percent
Tightened considerably	0	0.0
Tightened somewhat	1	4.5
Remained basically unchanged	19	86.4
Eased somewhat	2	9.1
Eased considerably	0	0.0
Total	22	100.0

d. Spreads of loan rates over your bank's cost of funds (wider spreads=tightened, narrower spreads=eased)

	All Respondents	
	Banks	Percent
Tightened considerably	0	0.0
Tightened somewhat	1	4.5
Remained basically unchanged	18	81.8
Eased somewhat	3	13.6
Eased considerably	0	0.0
Total	22	100.0

e. Premiums charged on riskier loans

	All Respondents	
	Banks	Percent
Tightened considerably	0	0.0
Tightened somewhat	2	9.1
Remained basically unchanged	17	77.3
Eased somewhat	3	13.6
Eased considerably	0	0.0
Total	22	100.0

f. Loan covenants

	All Respondents	
	Banks	Percent
Tightened considerably	0	0.0
Tightened somewhat	0	0.0
Remained basically unchanged	20	90.9
Eased somewhat	2	9.1
Eased considerably	0	0.0
Total	22	100.0

g. Collateralization requirements

	All Respondents	
	Banks	Percent
Tightened considerably	0	0.0
Tightened somewhat	0	0.0
Remained basically unchanged	22	100.0
Eased somewhat	0	0.0
Eased considerably	0	0.0
Total	22	100.0

h. Use of interest rate floors (more use=tightened, less use=eased)

	All Respondents	
	Banks	Percent
Tightened considerably	0	0.0
Tightened somewhat	0	0.0
Remained basically unchanged	19	95.0
Eased somewhat	1	5.0
Eased considerably	0	0.0
Total	20	100.0

3. If your bank has tightened or eased its credit standards or its terms for C&I loans or credit lines over the past three months (as described in questions 1 and 2), how important have been the following possible reasons for the change?

- A. Possible reasons for tightening credit standards or loan terms:

    a. Deterioration in your bank's current or expected capital position

    Responses are not reported when the number of respondents is 3 or fewer.

    b. Less favorable or more uncertain economic outlook

    Responses are not reported when the number of respondents is 3 or fewer.

    c. Worsening of industry-specific problems (please specify industries)

    Responses are not reported when the number of respondents is 3 or fewer.

    d. Less aggressive competition from other banks or nonbank lenders (other financial intermediaries or the capital markets)

    Responses are not reported when the number of respondents is 3 or fewer.

    e. Reduced tolerance for risk

    Responses are not reported when the number of respondents is 3 or fewer.

    f. Decreased liquidity in the secondary market for these loans

    Responses are not reported when the number of respondents is 3 or fewer.

    g. Deterioration in your bank's current or expected liquidity position

    Responses are not reported when the number of respondents is 3 or fewer.

    h. Increased concerns about the potential effects of legislative changes, supervisory actions, or accounting standards

    Responses are not reported when the number of respondents is 3 or fewer.

B. Possible reasons for easing credit standards or loan terms:

a. Improvement in your bank's current or expected capital position

	All Respondents	
	Banks	Percent
Not important	3	75.0
Somewhat important	1	25.0
Very important	0	0.0
Total	4	100.0

b. More favorable or less uncertain economic outlook

	All Respondents	
	Banks	Percent
Not important	2	50.0
Somewhat important	2	50.0
Very important	0	0.0
Total	4	100.0

c. Improvement in industry-specific problems (please specify industries)

	All Respondents	
	Banks	Percent
Not important	3	75.0
Somewhat important	0	0.0
Very important	1	25.0
Total	4	100.0

d. More aggressive competition from other banks or nonbank lenders (other financial intermediaries or the capital markets)

	All Respondents	
	Banks	Percent
Not important	0	0.0
Somewhat important	0	0.0
Very important	4	100.0
Total	4	100.0

e. Increased tolerance for risk

	All Respondents	
	Banks	Percent
Not important	2	50.0
Somewhat important	2	50.0
Very important	0	0.0
Total	4	100.0

f. Increased liquidity in the secondary market for these loans

	All Respondents	
	Banks	Percent
Not important	3	75.0
Somewhat important	1	25.0
Very important	0	0.0
Total	4	100.0

g. Improvement in your bank's current or expected liquidity position

	All Respondents	
	Banks	Percent
Not important	4	100.0
Somewhat important	0	0.0
Very important	0	0.0
Total	4	100.0

h. Reduced concerns about the potential effects of legislative changes, supervisory actions, or accounting standards

	All Respondents	
	Banks	Percent
Not important	4	100.0
Somewhat important	0	0.0
Very important	0	0.0
Total	4	100.0

4. Apart from normal seasonal variation, how has demand for C&I loans changed over the past three months? (Please consider only funds actually disbursed as opposed to requests for new or increased lines of credit.)

	All Respondents	
	Banks	Percent
Substantially stronger	0	0.0
Moderately stronger	2	8.7
About the same	18	78.3
Moderately weaker	3	13.0
Substantially weaker	0	0.0
Total	23	100.0

5. If demand for C&I loans has strengthened or weakened over the past three months (as described in question 4), how important have been the following possible reasons for the change?

   A. If stronger loan demand (answer 1 or 2 to question 4), possible reasons:

   a. Customer inventory financing needs increased

   Responses are not reported when the number of respondents is 3 or fewer.

   b. Customer accounts receivable financing needs increased

   Responses are not reported when the number of respondents is 3 or fewer.

   c. Customer investment in plant or equipment increased

   Responses are not reported when the number of respondents is 3 or fewer.

   d. Customer internally generated funds decreased

   Responses are not reported when the number of respondents is 3 or fewer.

   e. Customer merger or acquisition financing needs increased

   Responses are not reported when the number of respondents is 3 or fewer.

   f. Customer borrowing shifted to your bank from other bank or nonbank sources because these other sources became less attractive

   Responses are not reported when the number of respondents is 3 or fewer.

   g. Customers' precautionary demand for cash and liquidity increased

   Responses are not reported when the number of respondents is 3 or fewer.

B. If weaker loan demand (answer 4 or 5 to question 4), possible reasons:

   a. Customer inventory financing needs decreased

   Responses are not reported when the number of respondents is 3 or fewer.

   b. Customer accounts receivable financing needs decreased

   Responses are not reported when the number of respondents is 3 or fewer.

   c. Customer investment in plant or equipment decreased

   Responses are not reported when the number of respondents is 3 or fewer.

   d. Customer internally generated funds increased

   Responses are not reported when the number of respondents is 3 or fewer.

   e. Customer merger or acquisition financing needs decreased

   Responses are not reported when the number of respondents is 3 or fewer.

   f. Customer borrowing shifted from your bank to other bank or nonbank sources because these other sources became more attractive

   Responses are not reported when the number of respondents is 3 or fewer.

   g. Customers' precautionary demand for cash and liquidity decreased

   Responses are not reported when the number of respondents is 3 or fewer.

6. At your bank, apart from normal seasonal variation, how has the number of inquiries from potential business borrowers regarding the availability and terms of new credit lines or increases in existing lines changed over the past three months? (Please consider only inquiries for additional or increased C&I lines as opposed to the refinancing of existing loans.)

	All Respondents	
	Banks	Percent
The number of inquiries has increased substantially	0	0.0
The number of inquiries has increased moderately	2	8.7
The number of inquiries has stayed about the same	18	78.3
The number of inquiries has decreased moderately	3	13.0
The number of inquiries has decreased substantially	0	0.0
Total	23	100.0

Recent declines in oil prices may have led to strains in firms involved in oil and natural gas drilling/extraction and in the companies that provide support to those firms. Question 7 asks you to indicate what fraction of C&I loans held on your books are made to firms in the oil and natural gas drilling/extraction sector. Question 8 asks about your outlook for delinquencies and charge-offs on such loans. Question 9 asks about changes in credit policies made by your bank in response to developments in the oil and natural gas drilling/extraction sector.

7. Approximately what fraction of C&I loans currently outstanding on your bank's books were made to firms in the oil and natural gas drilling/extraction sector?

	All Respondents	
	Banks	Percent
More than 30 percent	0	0.0
More than 20 but less than 30 percent	0	0.0
More than 10 but less than 20 percent	9	45.0
Less than 10 percent	11	55.0
Total	20	100.0

For this question, 1 respondent answered "My bank does not make loans or extend lines of credit to firms in the oil and natural gas drilling/extraction sector."

8. Assuming that economic activity progresses in line with consensus forecasts, and energy commodity prices evolve in line with current future prices, what is your outlook for delinquencies and charge-offs on your bank's loans to firms in the oil and natural gas drilling/extraction sector over the remainder of 2015?

	All Respondents	
	Banks	Percent
Loan quality is likely to improve substantially	0	0.0
Loan quality is likely to improve somewhat	2	10.0
Loan quality is likely to remain around current levels	9	45.0
Loan quality is likely to deteriorate somewhat	9	45.0
Loan quality is likely to deteriorate substantially	0	0.0
Total	20	100.0

For this question, 1 respondent answered "My bank does not hold loans to firms in the oil and natural gas drilling/extraction sector."

9. Please indicate how important each of the following actions are in your bank's efforts to mitigate risks of loan losses from loans made to firms in the oil and natural gas drilling/extraction sector. (Please rate *each* possible action using the following scale: 1=not important, 2=somewhat important, 3=very important).

    a. Tightening underwriting policies on new loans or lines of credit made to firms in this sector

	All Respondents	
	Banks	Percent
Not important	3	15.0
Somewhat important	11	55.0
Very important	6	30.0
Total	20	100.0

b. Enforcing material adverse change clauses or other convenants to limit draws on existing credit lines to firms in this sector

	All Respondents	
	Banks	Percent
Not important	8	40.0
Somewhat important	8	40.0
Very important	4	20.0
Total	20	100.0

c. Reducing the size of existing credit lines to firms in this sector

	All Respondents	
	Banks	Percent
Not important	3	15.0
Somewhat important	8	40.0
Very important	9	45.0
Total	20	100.0

d. Restructuring outstanding loans to make them more robust to the revised outlook for energy prices

	All Respondents	
	Banks	Percent
Not important	8	40.0
Somewhat important	6	30.0
Very important	6	30.0
Total	20	100.0

e. Requiring additional collateral to better secure loans or credit lines to firms in this sector

	All Respondents	
	Banks	Percent
Not important	7	35.0
Somewhat important	9	45.0
Very important	4	20.0
Total	20	100.0

f. Tightening underwriting policies on new loans or credit lines made to firms in other sectors

	All Respondents	
	Banks	Percent
Not important	14	70.0
Somewhat important	6	30.0
Very important	0	0.0
Total	20	100.0

Questions 10-11 ask about commercial real estate (CRE) loans at your bank, including construction and land development loans and loans secured by nonfarm nonresidential real estate. Question 10 deals with changes in your bank's standards over the past three months. Question 11 deals with changes in demand. If your bank's lending standards or terms have not changed over the relevant period, please report them as unchanged even if they are either restrictive or accommodative relative to longer-term norms. If your bank's standards or terms have tightened or eased over the relevant period, please so report them regardless of how they stand relative to longer-term norms. Also, please report changes in enforcement of existing standards as changes in standards.

10. Over the past three months, how have your bank's credit standards for approving applications for CRE loans changed?

	All Respondents	
	Banks	Percent
Tightened considerably	0	0.0
Tightened somewhat	1	8.3
Remained basically unchanged	10	83.3
Eased somewhat	1	8.3
Eased considerably	0	0.0
Total	12	100.0

11. Apart from normal seasonal variation, how has demand for CRE loans changed over the past three months?

	All Respondents	
	Banks	Percent
Substantially stronger	0	0.0
Moderately stronger	3	25.0
About the same	7	58.3
Moderately weaker	2	16.7
Substantially weaker	0	0.0
Total	12	100.0

12. Over the past year, how has your bank changed the following policies on CRE loans? (Please assign *each* policy a number between 1 and 5 using the following scale: 1=tightened considerably, 2=tightened somewhat, 3=remained basically unchanged, 4=eased somewhat, 5=eased considerably.)

   a. Maximum loan size

	All Respondents	
	Banks	Percent
Tightened considerably	0	0.0
Tightened somewhat	1	9.1
Remained basically unchanged	8	72.7
Eased somewhat	2	18.2
Eased considerably	0	0.0
Total	11	100.0

   b. Maximum loan maturity

	All Respondents	
	Banks	Percent
Tightened considerably	0	0.0
Tightened somewhat	0	0.0
Remained basically unchanged	11	100.0
Eased somewhat	0	0.0
Eased considerably	0	0.0
Total	11	100.0

c. Spreads of loan rates over your bank's cost of funds (wider spreads=tightened; narrower spreads=eased)

	All Respondents	
	Banks	Percent
Tightened considerably	0	0.0
Tightened somewhat	0	0.0
Remained basically unchanged	5	45.5
Eased somewhat	5	45.5
Eased considerably	1	9.1
Total	11	100.0

d. Loan-to-value ratios

	All Respondents	
	Banks	Percent
Tightened considerably	0	0.0
Tightened somewhat	0	0.0
Remained basically unchanged	10	90.9
Eased somewhat	1	9.1
Eased considerably	0	0.0
Total	11	100.0

e. Debt-service coverage ratios

	All Respondents	
	Banks	Percent
Tightened considerably	0	0.0
Tightened somewhat	0	0.0
Remained basically unchanged	10	90.9
Eased somewhat	1	9.1
Eased considerably	0	0.0
Total	11	100.0

f. Market areas served (reduced market areas=tightened; expanded market areas=eased)

	All Respondents	
	Banks	Percent
Tightened considerably	0	0.0
Tightened somewhat	0	0.0
Remained basically unchanged	10	90.9
Eased somewhat	1	9.1
Eased considerably	0	0.0
Total	11	100.0

13. If your bank has tightened or eased its credit policies on CRE loans over the past year (as described in question 12), please select the 4 most important reasons among all the possible reasons listed below and rank them in order of importance. (Please respond to either 13A, 13B, or both as appropriate and rank the 4 most important reasons using a scale ranging from 4=the most important to 1=the least important.)

   A. Possible reasons for tightening credit policies on CRE loans over the past year:

   Responses are not reported when the number of respondents is 3 or fewer.

   B. Possible reasons for easing credit policies on CRE loans over the past year:

	All Respondents Mean
More favorable or less uncertain outlook for CRE property prices	4.0
More favorable or less uncertain outlook for vacancy rates or other fundamentals on CRE properties	2.8
More favorable or less uncertain capitalization rates (the ratio of current net operating income to the original sale price or current market value) on CRE properties	3.0
More aggressive competition from other banks or non-bank lenders (other financial intermediaries or the capital markets)	2.0
Increased tolerance for risk	3.0
Increased ability to securitize CRE loans	-
Decreased concerns about capital adequacy, liquidity position, or regulation more broadly	1.0
Other	1.0
Number of respondents	5

14. For each of the following categories of CRE lending, and assuming economic activity progresses in line with consensus forecasts, please indicate how you expect your bank's pace of loan originations during 2015 will change relative to its pace in 2014. (Please assign to *each* category a number between 1 and 6 using the following scale: 1=I expect the pace of originations at my bank will decline substantially; 2=I expect the pace of originations at my bank will decline somewhat; 3=I expect the pace of originations at my bank will be about the same; 4=I expect the pace of originations at my bank will increase somewhat; 5=I expect the pace of originations at my bank will increase substantially; 6=My bank does not originate this type of loan.)

a. Loans secured by nonfarm nonresidential properties

	All Respondents	
	Banks	Percent
I expect the pace of originations at my bank will decline substantially	0	0.0
I expect the pace of originations at my bank will decline somewhat	1	8.3
I expect the pace of originations at my bank will be about the same	4	33.3
I expect the pace of originations at my bank will increase somewhat	4	33.3
I expect the pace of originations at my bank will increase substantially	1	8.3
My bank does not originate this type of loan	2	16.7
Total	12	100.0

b. Loans secured by multifamily (5 or more) residential properties

	All Respondents	
	Banks	Percent
I expect the pace of originations at my bank will decline substantially	0	0.0
I expect the pace of originations at my bank will decline somewhat	0	0.0
I expect the pace of originations at my bank will be about the same	6	54.5
I expect the pace of originations at my bank will increase somewhat	1	9.1
I expect the pace of originations at my bank will increase substantially	1	9.1
My bank does not originate this type of loan	3	27.3
Total	11	100.0

c. 1-4 family residential construction loans

	All Respondents	
	Banks	Percent
I expect the pace of originations at my bank will decline substantially	0	0.0
I expect the pace of originations at my bank will decline somewhat	0	0.0
I expect the pace of originations at my bank will be about the same	3	27.3
I expect the pace of originations at my bank will increase somewhat	0	0.0
I expect the pace of originations at my bank will increase substantially	0	0.0
My bank does not originate this type of loan	8	72.7
Total	11	100.0

d. Other construction loans and all land development and other land loans

	All Respondents	
	Banks	Percent
I expect the pace of originations at my bank will decline substantially	0	0.0
I expect the pace of originations at my bank will decline somewhat	1	8.3
I expect the pace of originations at my bank will be about the same	4	33.3
I expect the pace of originations at my bank will increase somewhat	2	16.7
I expect the pace of originations at my bank will increase substantially	1	8.3
My bank does not originate this type of loan	4	33.3
Total	12	100.0

1. As of December 31, 2014, the 23 respondents had combined assets of $1.3 trillion, compared to $2.5 trillion for all foreign related banking institutions in the United States. The sample is selected from among the largest foreign-related banking institutions in those Federal Reserve Districts where such institutions are common.

www.ingramcontent.com/pod-product-compliance
Lightning Source LLC
Chambersburg PA
CBHW081204180526
45170CB00006B/2210